Missouri Compromise

LANDMARK LEGISLATION

Missouri Compromise

Susan Dudley Gold

Marshall Cavendish
Benchmark
New York

*Dedicated to Earlene Ahlquist Chadbourne, whose passion for
history continues to inspire me.*

*With special thanks to Catherine McGlone, Esq., for reviewing the text
of this book.*

Copyright © 2011 Susan Dudley Gold
Published by Marshall Cavendish Benchmark
An imprint of Marshall Cavendish Corporation
All rights reserved.

No part of this publication may be reproduced, stored in a retrieval system or transmitted,
in any form or by any means, electronic, mechanical, photocopying, recording, or otherwise,
without the prior permission of the copyright owner. Request for permission should
be addressed to the Publisher, Marshall Cavendish Corporation, 99 White Plains Road,
Tarrytown, NY 10591. Tel: (914) 332-8888, fax: (914) 332-1888.
Website: www.marshallcavendish.us
This publication represents the opinions and views of the author based on her personal
experience, knowledge, and research. The information in this book serves as a general
guide only. The author and publisher have used their best efforts in preparing this book and
disclaim liability rising directly and indirectly from the use and application of this book.

Other Marshall Cavendish Offices:
Marshall Cavendish International (Asia) Private Limited, 1 New Industrial Road, Singapore
536196 • Marshall Cavendish International (Thailand) Co. Ltd. 253 Asoke, 12th Flr,
Sukhumvit 21 Road, Klongtoey Nua, Wattana, Bangkok 10110, Thailand • Marshall
Cavendish (Malaysia) Sdn Bhd, Times Subang, Lot 46, Subang Hi-Tech Industrial Park, Batu
Tiga, 40000 Shah Alam, Selangor Darul Ehsan, Malaysia
Marshall Cavendish is a trademark of Times Publishing Limited

All websites were available and accurate when this book was sent to press.

Library of Congress Cataloging-in-Publication Data
Gold, Susan Dudley.
The Missouri Compromise / by Susan Dudley Gold.
p. cm. – (Landmark legislation)
Includes bibliographical references and index.
ISBN 978-1-60870-041-7 (alk. paper)
1. Missouri compromise–Juvenile literature. 2. Slavery–United States–History–Juvenile
literature. 3. United States–Politics and government–1815–1861–Juvenile literature. I. Title.
E373.G65 2011
973.5'4–dc22
2009032231

Publisher: Michelle Bisson
Art Director: Anahid Hamparian
Series Designer: Sonia Chaghatzbanian
Photo research by Candlepants, Inc.

The photographs in this book are used by permission and through the courtesy of: Library
of Congress: cover, 2, 3, 30, 35, 65, 89, 95, 120; The Granger Collection, New York: 6; Gilder
Lehrman Collection: 12; Getty Images: 14, 17; Hulton Archive, 20; Time Life Pictures/
War Department/National Archives/Time Life Pictures, 45; MPI, 50; Stock Montage, 69;
Kean Collection, 110; The Image Works: Photo12, 61; akg-images, 105; North Wind Picture
Archive: 82; New York Public Library: Astor, Lenox and Tilden Foundations, 114.

Cover: Daniel Webster addressing the Senate during the Missouri Compromise debate.

Printed in Malaysia(T)
1 3 5 6 4 2

Contents

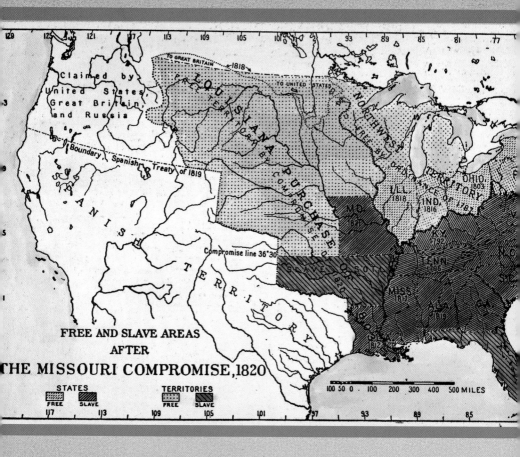

This map shows the division between free and slave areas of the United States after the Missouri Compromise was adopted in 1820 and Missouri was admitted to the Union in 1821. The yellow areas are free states, and the brown areas are slave states. Red indicates territories in which slavery was allowed; green shows free territories.

A Temporary Fix

In 1800 the United States occupied a thin strip of land running from the Atlantic Ocean west to the Ohio River. By the turn of the century three states—Vermont, Kentucky, and Tennessee—had joined the original thirteen to make up the new nation. Ohio became the seventeenth state in 1803.

With the Louisiana Purchase of 1803 the United States doubled its territory overnight with land bought from the French for a mere $15 million. Under the terms of the treaty that confirmed the sale, residents of the territory became citizens of the United States. The vast territory—which one day would comprise thirteen states—lured adventurous Americans to move west. Among those relocating to the new region were plantation owners from the South seeking richer soil for their crops. Within just a few years they began migrating with their slaves to the wild lands of the West.

The presence of slaves in the new territory sparked a fierce battle over whether slavery should be allowed outside of the

South. Sixteen years after the Louisiana Purchase the controversy over slavery ignited when Missouri applied to become a state. Slaveholders in the region demanded that slavery be allowed in states formed from lands obtained through the Louisiana Purchase. Northerners and others opposed to slavery resisted the addition of another state in which slavery would be legal. At the time eleven states allowed slavery and eleven states banned it. Admitting Missouri as a slave state would tip the balance between slave states and free states.

The dispute threatened to rip the nation apart. For months Congress conducted a bitter debate that explored the institution of slavery and its role in a nation based on equality and freedom. The controversy focused attention on the Constitution, which guaranteed life and liberty on one hand and allowed, but never mentioned, slavery on the other. It also presented leaders with the challenge of preserving the rights of individual states while maintaining a unified nation. Under the rules for statehood new states entered the Union with all the rights and privileges of the original thirteen states. But the original states themselves had different, and radically opposing, rules when it came to slavery.

Forging an agreement that served such opposite positions proved to be extremely difficult. It seemed that no compromise could bridge the gulf between slave states and free states. Thomas Jefferson, among others, believed the United States might well dissolve over the slavery question. He viewed the Missouri controversy as a "mere party trick" that had been designed by northerners who favored a strong federal government.

Congress averted a civil war, temporarily, when it adopted the Missouri Compromise in 1820 and related legislation the following year. The compromise created two new states;

Missouri was admitted to the Union as a slave state, and Maine was admitted as a state in which slavery was banned. The key element of the pact—Section 8—established the boundary between future slave states and free states in the territory acquired through the Louisiana Purchase. The boundary, which ran westward along the southern border of Missouri, set the dividing line at 36° 30′ northern latitude. Under the agreement slavery was allowed in the areas south of the line and banned in areas north of the line. Slavery was also allowed in Missouri, which lay north of the line. The compromise essentially isolated slavery to the region below the 36° 30′ latitude line (with the exception of Missouri).

Although the Missouri Compromise managed to keep the peace, its terms pleased neither side in the controversy. The pact angered southerners, who clung to the doctrine of states' rights and disputed Congress's right to override local support for slavery. Northerners protested the expansion of slavery into Missouri and the southern half of the Louisiana Territory. Bitterness over the legislation continued to simmer until 1854, when Congress repealed the compromise and allowed the citizens of the Kansas and Nebraska territories to decide whether to allow slavery within their borders. Three years later the U.S. Supreme Court ruled, in the *Dred Scott* decision, that Congress had no power to ban slavery. Under the ruling the Missouri Compromise became unconstitutional.

The Union dissolved along with the Missouri Compromise. "The repeal of the Missouri Compromise made the Civil War inevitable," according to historian Robert Pierce Forbes. For more than three decades the Missouri Compromise had been the glue holding the clashing sections of the country together. During that time abolitionists pushed to free the slaves, but

Missouri Compromise

SEC. 8. And be it further enacted. That in all that territory ceded by France to the United States, under the name of Louisiana, which lies north of thirty-six degrees and thirty minutes north latitude, not included within the limits of the state, contemplated by this act, slavery and involuntary servitude, otherwise than in the punishment of crimes, whereof the parties shall have been duly convicted, shall be, and is hereby, forever prohibited: Provided always, That any person escaping into the same, from whom labour or service is lawfully claimed, in any state or territory of the United States, such fugitive may be lawfully reclaimed and conveyed to the person claiming his or her labor or service as aforesaid.

APPROVED, March 6, 1820.

the existence of the free state/slave state line set by the Missouri Compromise gave Congress a reason to avoid the issue. Advocates on both sides of the conflict accepted the line as settled law. By repealing the pact, Congress and the Supreme Court abandoned the spirit of compromise and eliminated any common ground based in law. There was no longer any peaceful means of bringing together the two extremes for and against slavery. The tensions that the Missouri Compromise had defused forty years earlier finally erupted in 1861, propelling the nation into the Civil War.

CHAPTER ONE

Westward Ho!

The American Revolution bound together thirteen strong, independent colonies that joined forces to fight a common enemy. Once the war ended, however, the victorious colonies found they had very real differences among themselves. The economy of the wealthy southern colonies revolved around large plantations devoted to agriculture that were dependent on slave labor. Although some northerners had slaves, the economies of the northern colonies did not depend on slavery but on trade, small farms, and a diverse mix of businesses.

During the Revolutionary War the colonies formed a loose coalition that allowed each one to direct its own affairs. For the first few years after winning independence from England, the country continued to operate as a confederacy of separate states. The Articles of Confederation, which the founders had drawn up during the Revolutionary War, established a federal government but gave it few

The Colonization Society's president was James Madison, who became the fourth president of the United States. The certificate pictured above was given to those who joined the society.

powers. Under the articles the federal government could not enforce laws, levy taxes, or make treaties unless all the states agreed. Each state could issue its own paper money, determine how to deal with the Indian tribes living within its boundaries, and engage in trade wars with other states and foreign countries.

Many leaders soon realized that a strong federal government was needed to determine the new country's course. They believed that if individual states continued to pull in different directions, each according to its own agenda, the fledgling nation would not thrive. This division of power became a major source of controversy among leaders of the United States. In a convention held in May 1787, the nation's founders forged a set of rules governing the country as a whole. The result, the U.S. Constitution, created a strong central government and detailed in seven articles how the country would be run. On September 17, 1787, thirty-nine of the forty-two delegates attending the convention signed the Constitution. The document became the law of the land on June 21, 1788, after New Hampshire became the ninth state to ratify it. Members of the first federal Congress of the United States took office in 1789. More than two years later, on December 15, 1791, the Bill of Rights went into effect as a safeguard to protect individuals' and states' rights against a powerful federal government.

The new system of government divided power among three branches: Congress (legislative), the president (executive), and the Supreme Court (judicial). Each branch guards against a takeover of power by any other branch. The president, as representative of all the American people, serves as head of state. Congress, made up of representatives from each state, writes the laws. The Supreme Court acts as guardian of the law and ensures that the government operates according to the provisions of the Constitution.

NORTHWEST ORDINANCE OF 1787

Even before the founders approved the Constitution, leaders wrestled with the question of how to deal with new territory as the nation expanded. In 1787 they adopted a document called the Northwest Ordinance that set out terms of government for the lands in the northwest portion of the Ohio River valley. This land would later encompass the states of Ohio,

Thomas Jefferson, though himself a slaveholder, persuaded the nation's founders not to allow slavery in the territories northwest of the original thirteen states.

Indiana, Illinois, Michigan, and Wisconsin. Thomas Jefferson, a slaveholder himself, managed to persuade his colleagues to accept a ban on slavery in the newly ceded territory. The ordinance set up a general assembly to rule the territory and spelled out the conditions under which new states would be admitted to the Union.

Regions with at least five thousand free adult males could elect representatives to the General Assembly. Such areas would be allowed one representative per five hundred adult male residents. Residents could apply for admission to the Union when the population in their region reached sixty thousand.

The Second Continental Congress unanimously passed the Northwest Ordinance of 1787 on July 13. The ordinance broke ground by setting up the first organized territory of the United States. It also established that the federal government rather than the states would direct the nation's westward expansion. Slavery was absolutely banned in the Northwest Territory, but the ordinance ordered the return of fugitive slaves who sought refuge in the region.

Under the terms of the ordinance the entire Northwest Territory could be divided into no less than three and no more than five states. Those new states were to be admitted to the Union "on an equal footing with the original States in all respects whatever." Citizens of each new state would be free to set up their own constitution and government, provided that they adopted a "republican" system. By "republican" the founders meant a government that conformed to "the fundamental principles of civil and religious liberty."

After the adoption of the U.S. Constitution, the Continental Congress became the U.S. Congress. One of Congress's first acts was to ensure that the Northwest Ordinance remained in effect. The prohibition against slavery in the Northwest Territory held fast for the sixty-one years it took for all of the region to achieve statehood. Five new free states carved from the territory joined the Union in the following decades. Wisconsin, the last portion of the region to become a member of the Union, joined as a free state in 1848. This ultimately increased the power of antislavery advocates in Congress and gave an edge to supporters of the Union during the days leading up to the Civil War.

LOUISIANA PURCHASE: DEAL OF THE CENTURY

The end of the eighteenth century was a time of monumental changes in the world order. The British colonists in North America broke away from England in a bloody revolution to form the United States, a new, independent nation. The French followed suit, deposing their king and setting up a republic with a military general, Napoleon Bonaparte, as leader. Under Napoleon, French armies conquered much of Europe. England, with its still-mighty navy, stood fast against its longtime enemy, fighting for control over what remained of its vast colonial empire.

During the Napoleonic Wars, which ravaged Europe in the early 1800s, France won control of Spanish holdings in North America that included Louisiana and surrounding lands west of the Mississippi River. As part of his plan to control lucrative West Indies trade routes, Napoleon sought to take over Haiti, then known as Saint-Domingue, which occupied the western half of the Caribbean island of Hispaniola. The French leader envisioned shipping Haiti's coffee, sugar, cotton, and indigo to the Louisiana port of New Orleans for distribution throughout the world.

French troops led by Napoleon's brother-in-law, General Charles Victor Emmanuel Leclerc, arrived in Saint-Domingue in January 1802. Determined to take over the island nation, they fought an equally determined resistance army of former slaves led by François Dominique Toussaint L'Ouverture. Toussaint, himself a former slave, inspired his poorly equipped forces to fight the French, even after being captured and imprisoned. Nearly 30,000 French soldiers and sailors lost their lives in the conflict and to the yellow fever epidemic that followed. Leclerc was among those stricken by the deadly disease. After Leclerc's death, one of Toussaint's

Toussaint L'Ouverture, a former slave, led the resistance to the attempt by France to take over Haiti. The resistance succeeded, though L'Ouverture was captured.

generals, Jean-Jacques Dessalines, seized control of the colony. The resistance of the island's inhabitants, disease, escalating losses of men and money, attacks by the British, and the devastation of Haiti's crops caused by the war put an end to Napoleon's West Indies trade scheme.

Napoleon's misfortunes became America's good luck. The fiasco in Haiti strained France's treasury and left Napoleon looking for ways to raise money to fund his ongoing conflicts with Britain. The Americans had been lobbying to buy New Orleans from France ever since learning that France had taken over ownership of the territory. Under orders from President Thomas Jefferson, Robert Livingston, America's minister to France, had asked about buying New Orleans and Florida (the latter still under Spanish control) in 1801. Despite repeated inquiries, Livingston made no progress; the French were not interested in discussing the matter at that time.

With the failed mission in Haiti destroying his plans for New Orleans, Napoleon shifted focus. Funds were in short supply for his latest European expeditions, and he had little desire to spend more money to defend New Orleans against the British. On April 11, 1803, Napoleon instructed François Barbé-Marbois, the French minister of the treasury, to open negotiations with the Americans. After haggling over the price for several days, both sides agreed that the United States would pay France $15 million for the entire Louisiana Territory. James Monroe, who had been sent by Jefferson to negotiate the purchase, and Livingston signed the pact on May 8 or May 9. The entire document, including the French version signed by Barbé-Marbois, was predated April 30, 1803.

The exact boundaries of the purchase were never clearly set forth in the treaty, nor in a later pact that transferred ownership to the United States. The United States later claimed that West Florida was included in the territory, but both Spain and France disputed that assertion. Even without the Florida property, though, the new territory measured more than 500 million acres. The price per acre amounted to less than three cents. Covering a broad swath of land extending from the Mississippi River west to the Rocky Mountains, the property was larger than Great Britain, Germany, France, Spain, Portugal, and Italy combined. In little more than one hundred years the new region would be carved into thirteen states: Arkansas, Missouri, Iowa, Nebraska, South Dakota, almost all of Oklahoma and Kansas, and large parts of North Dakota, Montana, Wyoming, Minnesota, Colorado, and Louisiana. Many viewed the purchase as the deal of the century. Nineteenth-century historian Henry Adams characterized the Louisiana Purchase as "an event so portentous as to defy measurement" and declared that it "ranked in historical importance next to the Declaration of Independence and the adoption of the Constitution."

MANIFEST DESTINY

In 1804 Congress divided the newly purchased land into two sections. The parcel south of the 32nd parallel became the Territory of Orleans; the northern parcel became the District of Louisiana (later the Missouri Territory). Beginning in 1804 Meriwether Lewis and William Clark set out on a remarkable expedition covering more than 8,000 miles across the Louisiana Territory to the West Coast and back. Their goal was to find a water route to the Pacific Ocean. Following instructions from President Jefferson, the two explorers recorded their journey in meticulous detail.

The expedition began at the mouth of the Missouri River,

Captain Clark & his men building a line of Huts

Lewis and Clark are still famed for their eight-thousand-mile expedition across the whole of the territory purchased from the French.

near St. Louis. From there the explorers sailed west on the Missouri to Kansas and on to Nebraska, South Dakota, North Dakota, and Montana. When the river ended at Great Falls, Montana, the explorers trekked across the Rocky Mountains and on to the Columbia River and the Pacific coast, along the borders of present-day Washington and Oregon. The return trip, which began in March 1806, ended six months later in St. Louis. Sacagawea, a Shoshone woman who as a young girl had been taken captive by the French, interpreted for Lewis and Clark and helped smooth relations with the native tribes in the region.

Although they failed to find an intercontinental water route, Lewis and Clark succeeded in opening the territory to adventurous settlers. Their reports included rich descriptions of the land, the native inhabitants, and the plants, animals, and other resources they found there. The maps they created of the vast territory guided the thousands of settlers eager to make their way west. By the time of Lewis and Clark's return trip through Missouri, a widow they had met there in the early days of the expedition had her plantation "under tollarable good way," and a friend of Clark's had settled in St. Louis and opened a tavern. As news of the Lewis and Clark expedition spread, farmers, adventurers, and entrepreneurs immediately began to pour into the new lands.

Captivated by the vast lands acquired through the Louisiana Purchase, many Americans embraced the belief that it was the United States' destiny to rule over a great domain. To fulfill that goal, Americans pushed westward, taming the wilderness and populating the lands between the Mississippi River and the Pacific Ocean with cities and towns. The duty to expand westward later became known as "manifest destiny." John L. O'Sullivan, the editor of the *Democratic Review* and the *New York Morning News*, coined the phrase in an 1845 article in which he proclaimed that nothing must prevent "the fulfillment of our manifest destiny to overspread the continent allotted by Providence for the free development of our yearly multiplying millions."

KING COTTON

Eli Whitney's invention of the cotton gin in 1793 set the stage for the mass migration that occurred after the Louisiana Purchase. The new machine allowed farmers to process cotton much more efficiently than could be done by hand. As a result southern plantation owners grew cotton on much more of their land than before. With so much land available to the west, farmers no longer needed to rotate crops to give portions of the land time to replenish its nutrients. Instead, farmers harvested their acreage until it was depleted. Once that occurred, they moved west, taking their slaves with them and planting cotton on huge plots in the new territory. Younger sons who did not inherit land also migrated to claim their own plots in the undeveloped territories to the west.

In 1791 the United States produced 2 million pounds of cotton, only four-tenths of a percent of the amount produced worldwide. By 1831 almost half the world's supply of cotton came from the United States—385 million pounds annually. On the eve of the Civil War, in 1860, U.S. cotton production had skyrocketed to 1.65 billion pounds and accounted for 66 percent of the world's total. "Cotton literally exploded across the American frontier," according to Douglas R. Egerton, professor of history at Le Moyne College in Syracuse, New York. As the cotton crop boomed in the lands west of the Mississippi River, the number of slaves imported into the region increased.

STEPS TO END SLAVERY

In the late 1700s and early 1800s the United States and the world viewed slavery as an evil that eventually would become extinct. Even before becoming a state, Vermont adopted in 1777 the first American constitution to free the children of slaves once they became adults. Other northern states followed suit so that by the 1810s, a number of free blacks had begun to assert their independence in the North. The U.S. abolition movement got its official start in 1833 with the founding of the American Anti-Slavery Society. But

efforts to ban slavery in the United States began with settlers long before the nation was formed. Georgia's charter
forbade slavery, and early settlers there tried unsuccessfully
to keep slavery out of the colony. By the early 1800s northern abolitionists—those who wanted to eliminate slavery
altogether—were calling for the nation to free its slaves and
ban slavery forever.

Free blacks, however, posed a threat to whites in both the
North and the South. Despite popular support for emancipation in the North, most whites there did not envision themselves living and socializing with former slaves. Even those
who viewed free blacks as equals believed they would never
be granted full rights in the United States. Southern slaveholders feared that free blacks would inspire slaves to revolt
or try to escape. In 1816 the American Colonization Society
(ACS)—formed by slaveholders, Quakers, abolitionists, and
prominent white leaders including James Monroe and Henry
Clay—provided a way to deal with free blacks that people
on both sides endorsed: ship them to Africa. Beginning in
1820 several groups of free blacks sailed to Africa and set
up colonies. They called their new homeland Liberia, meaning "land of freedom." For the first twenty-two years white
agents of the ACS ran the country. In 1842 Joseph Jenkins
Roberts became the first black man to serve as governor of
Liberia. He became president when the country declared its
independence in 1847.

Jefferson, Clay, and, for a time, Abraham Lincoln promoted
the idea of deporting free blacks and resettling them in Liberia as a way to rid the nation of the dangers they posed. As
an alternative to emancipation, however, colonization was
impractical at best. The wholesale removal of American
blacks to Africa would have required millions of dollars and a

relocation operation of massive scale. Slaveholders forced to give up what they considered to be property would demand payment for the loss of their slaves, and the entire southern economic system—deprived of its slave labor—would have had to be restructured. Not all blacks, even slaves, embraced the idea. Many of the new generations of blacks in America, who had never lived in Africa, had little desire to move there.

Still, small steps were taken in the effort to end slavery. Following Britain's lead, the United States banned the importation of slaves in 1808. Many other nations banned the slave trade, and by the 1830s trafficking in African slaves was illegal everywhere in the world. While the United States technically prohibited the international slave trade, it sanctioned slavery and continued to allow the buying and selling of slaves already in the Americas. Under U.S. law blacks taken off illegal slave ships could be sold at market in southern states, where slavery was permitted.

The international slave-trade ban increased the demand and drove prices higher for domestic slaves. The planters migrating west brought their slaves with them or bought black workers from other slaveholders in the South. For plantation owners in Virginia and other farmers of the South whose lands were becoming depleted, their slaves accounted for much of their wealth. The western territory created a new market for their slaves, a sought-after commodity in the regions that allowed slavery.

The territories governed by the Northwest Ordinance, for the most part, remained free of slaves. The slave population in the territories to the south and southwest, favored by southern planters, steadily grew. By 1860 Mississippi had a greater percentage of blacks than any of the original southern states.

A QUESTION OF MONEY AND POWER

At the end of the 1700s almost 700,000 slaves lived in the United States, and almost all of them—94 percent—resided in the South (below the Mason-Dixon Line, separating Maryland and West Virginia from Pennsylvania and Delaware). If one considers that slaves worked at least sixty hours a week and averaged fifty-one weeks of work a year, their labor (more than 2 billion hours a year at the end of the 1700s) was of great value to southern landowners. Even at 10 cents an hour slave labor would have been valued at more than $200 million a year.

The majority of northerners grudgingly accepted what they called the South's "peculiar institution." Many northerners, while not slaveholders themselves, benefited from trade that depended on slavery. Northern factories manufactured cotton goods; banks in the North financed tobacco and sugar plantations. Shipbuilders provided vessels to transport southern goods, and merchants profited from trading in southern merchandise.

Abolitionists met with resistance and scorn in the North as well as the South. Even people opposed to slavery feared that abolishing it would damage the nation's economy and lead to violence, perhaps even war. Those fears and northern financial interests in slavery helped keep the split between North and South from widening further.

But as settlers in the territories west of the Mississippi River began pushing to set up their own states, the debate over slavery intensified. It soon became a central issue in the battle for power between North and South. Under the laws of the time slaves could not vote but counted in determining the number of representatives to Congress allotted each state. Five slaves were equal to three white men in the count for

U.S. Political Parties 1780–1860

Major Parties	Noted Members

Federalists, 1787–1815 — Alexander Hamilton
Beliefs: Strong central government, banking system, tariffs

Republicans (anti-Federalists), 1792 — Thomas Jefferson
Democratic-Republican Party, 1798–1815 — James Monroe
Beliefs: States' rights, right of states to overrule federal laws within state borders, economy based on farming

Democratic-Republican Party, 1815–1824 — James Madison
Beliefs: Adopted many of Federalists' policies

Democrats, 1824 — Andrew Jackson
Beliefs: Strong individual rights versus weak federal power, against federally funded infrastructure (roads, canals, etc.)

National Republicans, 1824–1833 — John Quincy Adams, Henry Clay
Beliefs: Strong federal government, infrastructure, tariffs

Whigs, 1834–1856 — Henry Clay, James Calhoun, Daniel Webster
Beliefs: Strong central government (Congress), national banking system, federal infrastructure (roads, waterways), national tariffs, split over expansion of slavery to territories

Republicans, 1854 — Abraham Lincoln
Beliefs: Opposed to slavery in territories, for Homestead Act to give land to new settlers in the West, for federal tariffs

Minor Parties	Noted Members

Anti-Masonic, 1828–1838 — William Wirt
Beliefs: For federal infrastructure, tariffs

Free-Soil Party, 1848–1854 — Martin Van Buren
Beliefs: Opposed to slavery in territories, for Homestead Act, federal tariffs , federally funded infrastructure

representatives and presidential electors. States with slaves, therefore, had a greater proportion of representatives per voter than did free states. Many northerners opposed the creation of new slave states not only on moral grounds but also because it would give voters in the South more power.

Those who favored a strong central government and those who lobbied for states' rights were also engaged in a struggle for power. After the War of 1812 the old Federalist Party of Alexander Hamilton's day was for the most part dead. The Federalists, who pushed for federal control in many areas, still held sway in some northern states, but their presidential candidate, Rufus King of New York, received only 34 electoral votes out of 218 cast in the 1816 race.

James Monroe, a Democratic-Republican, won the election. King, who had served as a delegate from Massachusetts to the Continental Congress and later became a noted abolitionist, was the last Federalist candidate to run for president. By the time of the Missouri Compromise, in 1820, only 26 Federalists of a total of 186 members served in the House of Representatives. Federalists held nine of the Senate's forty-six seats.

The Democratic-Republicans, under President Madison, adopted many of the Federalists' policies, including support for a strong central government, a national bank, and a federally controlled army. By the time James Monroe came to power in 1816, his Democratic-Republican supporters constituted the only party in town—or at least the only party of any consequence.

A faction of the Democratic-Republican Party clung to the earlier ideas promoted by Thomas Jefferson—that states reigned supreme. They believed that the federal government existed as a compact of the individual states and could act only with the consent of the states. Many southern politicians embraced the states' rights doctrine as a defense against federal (and northern) attempts to limit or end slavery.

A controversy over the national bank helped win more support for states against the federal government in the struggle for power. The national bank, which several states fiercely opposed, stimulated the move west by lending money to land speculators in the new territories. Farmers bought land and established large agricultural operations that supplied food to European and domestic markets. During this time, between 1815 and 1819, trade flourished, cotton prices soared, mills and factories employed thousands of workers, the population increased, and merchants prospered. The Era of Good Feeling, as the period was called, was one of peace, expansion, and profits.

The Panic of 1819 interrupted the prosperity. With the end of the European wars, farmers there began producing more crops and manufactured goods, causing prices to drop worldwide. U.S. farmers could not pay their loans, trade and new investments stopped, factories closed and people lost their jobs, cotton prices fell, and the national bank began foreclosure proceedings. This caused a huge outcry. Even before the panic Maryland had tried to shut down the bank by imposing a $15,000 tax on its operations in the state. After the bank refused to pay, the case went before the U.S. Supreme Court. On March 6, 1819, the Supreme Court weighed in on the side of Congress and the federal government when it ruled unanimously in favor of the federal bank. Chief Justice John Marshall issued the decision, which reinforced the supremacy of the national government over the states.

The public denounced both the ruling and the federal government. Many Americans blamed Congress and the national bank for the economic downturn. Some citizens supported a federal tariff to reduce foreign competition, while others called for a less powerful and less costly federal government. The panic and the ensuing depression, which lasted until 1823, deepened the split in the Democratic-Republican Party along sectional lines. Northerners and easterners stood on the side of federal tariffs to ease the situation, while westerners and southerners lined up behind efforts to let individual states handle their own affairs. The factions would also take opposite sides in the Missouri crisis, which would reach its climax in the midst of the panic.

St. Louis had grown from a small village to a major trading hub by 1859, when this scene was painted.

CHAPTER TWO

A Delicate Balance

In 1812 the Territory of Orleans petitioned to become a state, the first region gained through the Louisiana Purchase to do so. The area was populated by a mix of American Indians; French, Spanish, German, and English settlers; free blacks; and slaves. By 1810 more than 76,000 people lived in the Territory of Orleans, not counting the Indians in the region, who were not included in the census. About half of the population was black (including slaves and free blacks), and half was white.

The region, adopting the name Louisiana, was admitted into the Union as a slave state with little controversy. Slavery had existed in the area since the days of the French plantations. Since Louisiana was not part of the Northwest Territory, it did not fall under the ban on slavery set forth in the 1787 Ordinance, which applied to lands in the northwest section of the Ohio River valley. Louisiana did follow the ordinance's guidelines for becoming a state.

31

With the addition of Louisiana as a slave state, nine states permitted slavery, and nine others prohibited it. Over the next several years Congress began to pay closer attention to whether new territories would become slave states or free states. In 1816 Indiana joined the Union as a free state, followed the next year by Mississippi, a slave state, preserving the delicate balance between proslavery and antislavery forces in the Senate.

THE SETTLING OF MISSOURI

The first Europeans set foot on Missouri soil in 1673. Father Jacques Marquette, a Catholic priest, and Louis Joliet stopped to explore the region during their journey down the Mississippi River. In 1682 the adventurer René-Robert Cavalier, Sieur de La Salle, claimed the territory for France. Missouri, along with much of the Southwest, came under Spanish rule in 1762, under the terms of the Treaty of Fontainebleau.

After suffering disastrous losses in the Seven Years' War, Spain transferred its claims to the Louisiana Territory, including Missouri, to France in 1800. Three years later the entire parcel became the property of the United States, when Napoleon sold it for $15 million.

Early settlers in the region concentrated on the fur trade. The Mississippi River, which forms the eastern boundary of Missouri, and the Missouri River, which joins the Mississippi near St. Louis, provided a crossroads that brought settlers and trade into the territory. As the population grew, towns and cities sprang up along the waterways. The Indian tribes in the region, like those in other areas, soon were forced to relinquish their homelands and move farther west.

Pierre Laclède Liguest, a French businessman, predicted St. Louis would become "one of the finest cities in America" when he founded the settlement in 1764. The village, which would later develop into Missouri's largest metropolitan area, was established by French settlers after England claimed jurisdiction over settlements to the east. It took its name from the French king Louis IX. Centered around Laclède's trading post, St. Louis served as the launching site in 1804 of Lewis and Clark's groundbreaking expedition through the West. When the explorers returned two years later, the city became the "gateway to the West" for the masses ready to follow the new route into America's frontier. Adventurers, investors, mountaineers, and settlers streamed into the city to begin their western journey.

The invention of the steamboat further opened the area to trade. On July 27, 1817, St. Louis residents lined the Missouri River shore to watch as the first steamboat sailed into the harbor. Later, as many as one hundred steamboats would be tied up to the city's levee in a single day. In the decade between 1810 and 1820 Missouri's population grew from 20,000 whites to more than 66,000, according to the U.S. census. In 1820 approximately 10,000 slaves lived in Missouri; by 1860 that number had grown to almost 115,000.

After Louisiana joined the Union in 1812, Congress voted to change the name of the remaining area from the District of Louisiana to the Missouri Territory. The southern part of the Missouri Territory eventually became the state of Missouri, while the remaining portions were grouped together as unorganized territory. In 1819 the southwest section of the unorganized territory became the Arkansas Territory (later to become the states of Arkansas and Oklahoma). The rest of the unorganized territory eventually formed the states of Iowa, Kansas, Nebraska, Wyoming, Colorado, Montana, South Dakota, North Dakota, and part of Minnesota.

PETITION FOR STATEHOOD

On January 8, 1818, Speaker of the House of Representatives Henry Clay of Kentucky submitted to the fifteenth Congress the first bill to make Missouri a state. Following the procedure set up by the 1787 Northwest Ordinance, the initial bill asked only that Missouri be granted permission to form a government and develop a constitution. After Missouri fulfilled those duties, Congress would have to take another vote before the territory could officially become a state. Missouri's first bill reached the House on March 16, 1818, but representatives took no action on the petition before the session ended for the summer.

Missouri residents tried again for statehood during the next congressional session. On December 18, 1818, they submitted a second petition to the House. Like Louisiana, the Missouri Territory permitted slavery. Illinois had just been admitted as a free state, and many expected Missouri to win quick approval as a slave state. Debate on the matter began on February 13, 1819. James Tallmadge Jr., a representative from New York, ignited the controversy when he proposed a precedent-setting amendment to restrict slavery in Missouri. The measure called on Congress to bar the importation of additional slaves to Missouri and to require that children of slaves already living there be freed at age twenty-five.

Tallmadge's amendment aroused immediate hostility from proponents of slavery, "like a firebell in the night," as Thomas Jefferson would later describe it. The aging statesman, nearly eighty at the time of the dispute, said the controversy filled him with terror. "I considered it at once as the knell of the Union," he wrote a friend in April 1820.

The dilemma that Missouri's petition presented, extending slavery to the new territory as the South asked or banning

Speaker of the House Henry Clay submitted the bill that would make Missouri a state. In the ensuing free- versus slave-state debate, he argued that each state should be able to decide for itself whether to allow slavery within its borders.

it as the North wanted, was like holding "a wolf by the ears," Jefferson wrote. "We can neither hold him, nor safely let him go. Justice is in one scale, and self-preservation in the other."

Antislavery forces in the North adamantly opposed Missouri's statehood petition, which if granted would allow slavery to spread farther west. They feared Missouri's admittance to the Union as a slave state might serve as a model for the remaining territories located west of the Mississippi. The controversy that erupted over the issue divided the nation, pitting southerners against northerners. Abraham Lincoln, reflecting on the situation many years later, related how "threats of breaking up the Union were freely made; and the ablest public men of the day became seriously alarmed." The dispute, according to Lincoln, marked "the first great slavery agitation in the nation."

Tallmadge's amendment triggered a bitter debate over slavery that raged for several days. The arguments swung between two points.

- Congress had the right to require new states seeking to join the Union to abide by certain conditions, among them that slavery was contrary to a democratic nation (supported by antislavery forces).
- Congress had no right to establish the rules of government for a state, as long as the state complied with the Constitution (supported by proslavery forces).

In the midst of the controversy, Congress approved Alabama's petition to join the Union with little debate. Alabama, like its neighbors, allowed slavery. On March 2, 1819, Congress authorized Alabama to draw up a constitution and establish a state government. It would join the Union in December 1819 as a slave state, returning the nation to a balance between slave states and free states.

The different treatment Missouri and Alabama received

revolved around their locations. Alabama, surrounded by slave states, was located in the South, east of the Mississippi River. Missouri, on the other hand, abutted the free state of Illinois and lay much farther north and west of the Mississippi.

DESTINY OF MILLIONS

Representative John W. Taylor of New York began the House debate in February 1819 with arguments for the Tallmadge amendment and against the extension of slavery into the western regions. He noted that Congress's vote on the matter would affect far more than Missouri. The legislators would "decide the destiny of millions" when they set the rules for future states across the West. "Our votes this day," he told his fellow congressmen, "will determine whether the high destinies of this region, and of these generations, shall be fulfilled, or whether we shall defeat them by permitting slavery, with all its baleful consequences, to inherit the land."

The Constitution gave Congress the power to admit new states, and with that power came the right to require reasonable conditions for acceptance into the Union, Taylor argued. He noted that Congress had already required Ohio, Indiana, and Illinois to abide by the Northwest Ordinance of 1787, which barred slavery in those areas. "Missouri lies in the same latitude," Taylor said. "Its soil, productions, and climate are the same, and the same principles of government should be applied to it."

Opponents raised the issue that the earlier ordinance did not cover the lands of the Louisiana Purchase. Under the treaty of 1803 the inhabitants of the Louisiana Territory were guaranteed "all the rights, advantages and immunities of citizens of the United States." Proslavery forces argued that the treaty therefore granted Missourians and those living in the surrounding region the same right to own slaves as citizens in the southern states possessed. Taylor, however, objected to that interpretation. He contended that the treaty had no effect on petitions for statehood. It was up to Congress to determine whether a region became a state and to set the requirements for achieving statehood. To bolster his argument, Taylor reminded legislators that Congress had required Louisiana to fulfill certain conditions—among them the inclusion of trial by jury in its constitution—before allowing that state to join the Union. While Congress had only limited power over states, he said, it wielded total control over the territories, including whether to accept their petitions for statehood.

Speaker Clay argued just as forcefully that prospective states should be able to determine for themselves whether or not to allow slavery. He contended that the Constitution put new states on an equal footing with the original states. New as well as old states, he argued, had the power to set up their governments according to their own devices, as long as they did not violate the U.S. Constitution. That document, while not specifically addressing the issue of slavery, tolerated its existence and referred to slaves indirectly as those who were "held to Service or Labour in one State, under the Laws thereof."

Southerners bolstered Clay's arguments. P. P. Barbour, a representative from Virginia, argued that allowing some slaves to be brought to Missouri would spread out the enslaved population and make it more difficult for slaves to unite and rise against their masters. Barbour also claimed that placing a ban on slavery in Missouri and other western states would decrease the value of public lands there. And he repeated the South's contention that states, even prospective ones,

Slavery and the U.S. Constitution

The founders of the United States struggled mightily with the issue of slavery. Many of them owned slaves. Those who did not were well aware of the economic value of slaves to the fledgling nation's survival, particularly to the South, whose plantations relied on slave labor to harvest cotton, tobacco, and other crops. The slave trade also benefited northern shipbuilders, who provided vessels to transport slaves from Africa, and merchants, who profited from trade with the South and foreign countries (on the return trip to Africa).

On the other hand the founders viewed slavery as an evil institution, even if it was a necessary one. John Jay, a member of the Continental Congress and an advocate for a strong federal government, worked unsuccessfully to abolish slavery in New York and once wrote that he regretted not inserting a clause in the Constitution to end the institution.

Jay, a New York native whose father owned slaves, wrote, "It is much to be wished that slavery may be abolished. The honour of the States, as well as justice and humanity, in my opinion, loudly call upon them to emancipate these unhappy people. To contend for our own liberty, and to deny that blessing to others, involves an inconsistency not to be excused." Patrick Henry, the firebrand patriot of Virginia, called slavery a "lamentable evil" and expressed hope that leaders of the day would transmit to future generations "an abhorrence of slavery."

The international trade in slaves especially repelled the nation's early leaders. Most agreed it should be stopped as soon as possible, in the name of humanity and in light of the actions of other nations to ban it. Representatives of several southern states, however, resisted any move that would give the federal government power over state activities.

As a compromise between North and South the founders

agreed, in Section 9 of Article 1 of the Constitution, to tolerate the importation of African slaves until the year 1808. After that point Congress would be free to issue a ban on the international slave trade. The founders included other provisions in the Constitution to appease southern slaveholders. Section 2 of Article 4 required the return of fugitive slaves to their masters. The Constitution also accommodated the South by counting each slave as three-fifths of a free person when tallying a state's population to determine the federal taxes it would owe and the number of representatives it would have in Congress. The slaves, though, had no vote and no say in who represented the South in Congress. The counting system helped balance congressional representation between the populous northern states and the sparsely populated southern states.

Although these sections clearly referred to slaves, the Constitution did not make direct reference to slaves or slavery. Instead of using those words, the Constitution referred to "such Persons as any of the States now existing shall think proper to admit" when addressing the importation of slaves (Article 1, Section 9); a "Person held to Service or Labour in one State, under the Laws thereof, escaping into another," meaning a fugitive slave (Article 4, Section 2); and "all other Persons," as opposed to free persons, when figuring a state's population (Article 1, Section 2).

Abraham Lincoln suggested that the founders used the substitute phrases because they did not want to immortalize slavery in the Constitution. Instead, they chose to write about it in ambiguous terms that would allow future generations to ignore the fact that slavery had ever existed in the United States.

had ultimate power over their government. "This term State has a fixed and determinate meaning; in itself, it imports the existence of a political community, free and independent, and entitled to exercise all the rights of sovereignty, of every description whatever," he asserted. The Constitution, he contended, gave new states all the rights and privileges enjoyed by the original thirteen, including the right to allow slavery within their borders. Likewise, new states would have to follow certain practices, such as trial by jury, just as the original states did.

Northerners contended that slavery itself violated the principles of the republic touted in the Constitution. Representative Timothy Fuller of Massachusetts quoted the Declaration of Independence to make his point.

> We hold these truths to be self-evident, that all men are created equal, that they are endowed by their Creator with certain inalienable rights, that among these are life, liberty, and the pursuit of happiness.

Fuller reasoned that since slaves were undeniably men, those living in a "purely republican government" should by rights be "born free" and "entitled to liberty and the pursuit of happiness."

Several southern representatives objected, but Fuller continued. Slavery had been well-established when the nation was formed, he conceded; therefore, the South could not be expected to uproot it and threaten the region's existence. But, Fuller noted, to open the door to such a violation of republican government in new states would show flagrant disregard for the Constitution. "It clearly . . . is the duty of Congress, before admitting a new sister into the Union, to ascertain that her constitution or form of government is republican," Fuller said. Tallmadge's amendment barring slavery in Missouri, according to the Massachusetts lawmaker, merely ensured that the new state's government would follow the U.S. Constitution.

SLAVERY AS A "BENEFIT" TO BLACKS

The debate in Congress forced southerners to justify slavery to the rest of the nation. Until the Missouri controversy most southern lawmakers had described slavery as a "necessary evil" and had blamed their forefathers for introducing slaves to America. Since slavery was already in place when these southern landowners began running their plantations, they declared that they would have to put up with it.

The Missouri debate and the question of extending slavery into future states altered the South's defense of slavery. Representative Taylor challenged southerners to take the opportunity presented by Missouri's petition for statehood to avoid repeating the sins of their ancestors. "Gentlemen have now an opportunity of putting their principles into practice," Taylor intoned. "If they have tried slavery and found it a curse; if they desire to dissipate the gloom with which it covers their land; I call upon them to exclude it from the Territory in question [Missouri]; plant not its seeds in this uncorrupt soil; let not our children looking back to the proceedings of this day say of them as they have constrained to speak of their fathers, 'We wish their decision had been different; we regret the existence of this unfortunate population among us; but we found them here: we know not what to do with them; it is our misfortune, we must bear it with patience.'"

Southerners then tried to present slavery in a positive light.

For the first time these wealthy white men depicted slavery as a civilizing force. In the House, Speaker Clay argued that slavery freed white Americans from menial chores, thus allowing these supposedly superior beings to focus on more uplifting pastimes that advanced society. This school of thought also introduced the concept that the slaves themselves benefited from slavery because it allowed them to be exposed to white culture and Christianity.

"That was a new idea," according to history professor Douglas R. Egerton. "Men of Jefferson's generation never tried to pretend that slavery was a good thing for white or black. And certainly, Jefferson never had any interest in arguments that there was something civilizing about slavery, when it came to Africans."

During the debate in the Senate, Freeman Walker of Georgia claimed that northerners' perception of the treatment of slaves was wrong. "They hear the term slave, and their imaginations accompany it with nakedness, hunger, with the lash, the chain, and a destitution of every comfort," Walker said. "Nothing can be more foreign from the true condition of the slaves. As far as my knowledge extends, they are well clothed, well fed, and treated with kindness and humanity. They are cheerful and apparently happy." Senator William Smith of South Carolina agreed with Walker's assessment, contending that "there is no class of laboring people in any country upon the globe, except the United States, that are better clothed, better fed, or are more cheerful, or labor less, or who are more happy, or, indeed, who have more liberty and indulgence, than the slaves of the Southern and Western States."

Senator Benjamin Ruggles of Ohio expressed surprise that southerners had made such a radical change in their view of slavery. He noted that Smith justified slavery "on

Life as a Slave

Southerners such as Senator William Smith tried to paint a rosy picture of slavery, but his description of the treatment of slaves was far from the truth. Many plantation owners considered slaves to be a lower form of human and claimed it was their responsibility to guide and care for them. "Inspire a negro with perfect confidence in you and learn him to look to you for support and he is your slave," one slave owner declared. Many slave owners, however, used such paternal reassurances to conceal the extreme brutality that slaves endured. Photographs and testimony revealed vicious whippings that scarred backs and disfigured bodies. Other reports told of beatings, rapes, and savage attacks on slaves by their owners. Even those who escaped violence had to fulfill onerous chores, had no control over their lives or their families, and were forbidden by law from owning property or working on their own for pay.

Slaveholders rationed the food given to slaves. Servings were more plentiful on certain plantations than on others; some slaves suffered from malnutrition or went hungry. Few slaves had nutritious diets; most ate cornmeal, peas, molasses, lard, flour, and, occasionally, meat. Small gardens maintained by slaves provided some fresh greens and vegetables.

The type of clothing distributed to slaves depended on their jobs and whether they worked on field crews or in the house. Children often went naked, and those too old or sick to work at valuable jobs received only the barest essentials, with no extra outerwear to protect them in winter. Housing was also minimal. Most slaves lived in shacks with few amenities. Sometimes slaves who worked in the main house lived in spare rooms apart from the rest of the structure. Owners generally provided just enough care to keep slaves alive and healthy enough to work without spending extra money on their upkeep. Some slave families were allowed to stay together, but family members often were separated and sold to other plantation owners or transported to new

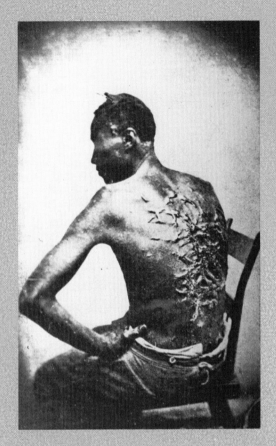

Though many southerners argued that slavery was a benign institution, it was anything but. This engraving of a slave with horrendous scars on his back from multiple whippings tells a truer, more realistic tale.

farmlands. Mothers and fathers were separated from their children, husbands and wives never saw one another again.

Until about the 1840s the majority of slaves worked on small plantations scattered throughout the South. These operations usually required between twenty and thirty slaves. Owners sometimes hired out extra workers to perform skilled labor in nearby towns. That gave slaves the chance to mix with other laborers, black and white. The owner collected payment for the slaves' services, but a skilled worker might also receive tips for his work. A few managed to save enough to buy their own freedom.

the broadest principles, without qualification or reserve." Such a stance, according to Ruggles, occupied "entirely new ground." Before the Missouri debate, he said, "slavery had not been considered as a matter of right, but as an evil, a misfortune entailed upon the country, for which no complete remedy could be suggested."

Speaker of the House Clay based his proslavery stance on what he called humanitarian reasons. If slaves were "dispersed over the country," he contended, they would be much better off than if they were concentrated in the South. The fertile new lands would allow plantation owners to provide their slaves with an abundance of food and other necessities. An unimpressed Taylor likened Clay's humanitarian argument to that of a do-gooder who saves a person's finger and then amputates the arm.

Proponents of Tallmadge's amendment presented a far less charitable view of slavery than the one described by Clay and the southerners. Representative Arthur Livermore of New Hampshire noted that slaves existed at the will of their masters. Their bodies could "be prostituted to any purpose, and deformed in any manner by their owners." Mothers and children were separated from each other and sold; laws forbade slaves from attending public worship services and learning to read. "How long will the desire of wealth render us blind to the sin of holding both the bodies and souls of our fellow men in chains!" he asked the lawmakers.

THREATS OF WAR

In its first vote on the measure the House passed Tallmadge's amendment 79 to 67. For two more days the full House debated Missouri's petition to join the Union "with considerable spirit," according to a report of the proceedings. At some points the discussion escalated to threats of war. Representative Thomas W. Cobb of Georgia warned that if Congress passed the measure with Tallmadge's amendment, "the Union will be dissolved." Casting a warning glance at Tallmadge, he told his fellow congressmen that "we have kindled a fire which all the waters of the ocean cannot put out, which seas of blood can only extinguish."

Tallmadge responded in kind. "If a dissolution of the Union must take place, let it be so! If civil war, which gentlemen so much threaten, must come, I can only say, let it come!" As a representative of the people of New York, Tallmadge pledged to "proclaim their hatred to slavery in every shape."

On February 16, 1819, the House voted 87 to 76 to pass the Tallmadge amendment restricting slavery in Missouri. A proposal to free slaves already living in what would become the new state when they reached the age of twenty-five also passed, with a vote of 82 to 78. The following day the House approved the Missouri statehood bill—"An act to authorize the people of the Missouri territory to form a constitution and state government, and for the admission of such state into the Union, on an equal footing with the original states"— along with the two amendments.

Even with a majority in the House, however, northern representatives failed to pass an amendment made by Representative Taylor to ban the importation of slaves into Arkansas Territory. Speaker of the House Clay cast the deciding vote against the amendment after a tie vote of 88 to 88. Some northerners believed they should give the South that territory, since it lay to the south of Kentucky and Missouri. "We must go on as we have begun; admitting some States with, and some without any restriction," said Ezekiel Whitman, a Massachusetts representative from the District of Maine.

Unbowed, Taylor offered a second amendment, proposing that slavery be banned north of a line along the 36° 30′ northern latitude. On a vote of 67 to 74, the House quickly defeated that proposal as well.

TO THE SENATE

The Senate's consideration of the Missouri bill later that month "gave rise to a long and animated debate," according to a report of the session. Senator James J. Wilson of New Jersey tried to postpone the matter until the next Congress, but his proposal met with defeat. Senators then voted 31 to 7 to strike out the House amendment that would have freed the children of slaves on their twenty-fifth birthday. The Senate also rejected the prohibition against bringing slaves into the new state by a narrower margin, 22 to 16. No further action on the bill was taken before the Senate adjourned for the day.

The following Monday, March 1, 1819, Senator James Burrill Jr. of Rhode Island proposed an amendment to the Missouri bill, just days before the end of the congressional session, that "the further introduction of slavery or involuntary servitude within the said territory, except for the punishment of crimes, be prohibited." The Senate, equally divided between slave states and free states, voted against the amendment. Fourteen supported limits on slavery; nineteen opposed the measure, including four senators from free states. Both senators from Illinois voted against the amendment; senators from Ohio and Indiana split their votes. The Senate then approved the Missouri bill without the amendments restricting slavery.

During the last days of the congressional session the Senate received word that the House would not agree to strike the slavery ban from the Missouri bill as the Senate had.

The Senate voted to stick to its own version of the bill and adjourned. Since the Senate version differed from the bill the House had passed, the measure did not become law. The controversy over slavery and Missouri's statehood would reappear in the next session during a divisive debate that once again evoked threats of civil war.

Though President James Monroe was publicly neutral in the debate, he worked tirelessly behind the scenes to effect a compromise.

CHAPTER THREE

Slave State, Free State

The sixteenth Congress opened amid ongoing tension over the extension of slavery and Missouri's desire to join the Union. On December 29, 1819, Senator William Smith of South Carolina presented Missouri's petition to become a state, outlining its boundaries and asking that the Senate grant residents the "rights, privileges, and immunities belonging to citizens of the United States." The petition, a duplicate of the one presented to the House in the last session, was quickly referred to the Senate Judiciary Committee for review.

MAINE'S CASE

At the same time that Missourians were lobbying to form a state, the citizens in the District of Maine, the northern section of Massachusetts, began petitioning to split from the commonwealth and become a separate state. The original settlers of Maine had established their own settlements, apart from the Puritans in neighboring Massachusetts Bay Colony. But when Oliver Cromwell and the Puritans took control of Britain in the 1650s, Massachusetts laid claim to the Province of Maine. Maine became part of Massachusetts, and Maine residents became citizens of the commonwealth.

The relationship between Maine and Massachusetts was a rocky one. Maine citizens chafed under Massachusetts taxes, the Puritan laws forced on them, and the government's preferential treatment of the church. As the northernmost district in Massachusetts, Maine received little attention and few resources from the commonwealth. During the War of 1812 Massachusetts refused to pay for local militias to defend the Maine coast. The lack of support infuriated Maine citizens and ignited the effort to seek independence from Massachusetts.

Separatists led by William King (half-brother of Rufus) rallied Maine citizens, who voted several times to set up their own state. Each time, the Massachusetts General Court rejected the idea. King and others worked to elect representatives to the Massachusetts General Court who would favor the independence movement. Maine, with a population of 300,000, provided more than one-third of the General Court's representatives, 145 out of a total of 402. Nine senators represented the district in the forty-member upper chamber in Boston.

The matter came to a head in the spring and summer of 1819. On June 19, 1819, the Massachusetts legislature finally agreed to allow Maine citizens to hold a vote on separating from the commonwealth. Proponents distributed flyers throughout Maine urging voters to support the move for independence. One such flyer posed the question "Shall Maine be a free, sovereign and independent State, or shall

you and your children remain forever the servants of a foreign power [Massachusetts]?"

On July 26, 1819, the citizens of Maine voted overwhelm-
ingly to separate from Massachusetts and become an independent state. Joining the Union as a free state had a double
meaning for many Mainers. To them, it meant being free
from Massachusetts rule as well as being a state free of slavery. The Massachusetts General Court voted to allow Maine
to seek statehood, but only with the proviso that the district
obtain permission from Congress by March 4, 1820, or Maine
would remain under Massachusetts control.

In October 1819 King and other delegates elected by
Maine voters held a convention in Portland. They voted to
keep "Maine" as the name of their new state and adopted
a state constitution. The delegates elected King as acting
governor. Maine citizens approved the new constitution on
January 6, 1820. The following April they elected King as the
state's first governor.

Representative John Holmes of Massachusetts presented
the Maine statehood bill to the House on December 8, 1819.
Because Maine had received permission from Massachusetts
for the split and had already formed a government and prepared a constitution, leaders skipped the first step and asked
Congress to approve its statehood directly. A few representatives expressed displeasure that Maine had not followed pro-
tocol and asked permission from Congress before setting up
a government and adopting a constitution. Mainers claimed
they had special status because they were not a territory
but part of Massachusetts, an original state. Apparently that
appeased the legislators, because the House referred the bill
to committee, which later released it for a vote. On January 3,
1820, the House approved Maine's request for statehood.

TWO STATES, ONE BILL

When the Maine bill came before the Senate, it was referred to the Judiciary Committee, which was also considering the Missouri bill. Senator William Smith of South Carolina chaired the committee. The members of the committee linked together the petitions of the two regions. On January 6, 1820, the committee sent Maine's petition to the full Senate with an amendment that authorized the citizens of Missouri to form a government and draw up a constitution. The report did not mention slavery, because the committee members assumed that Maine would be admitted as a free state, offsetting Missouri's status as a slave state. Southerners hoped that connecting the two bills would pressure the Senate into acting on Missouri's long-delayed request.

The move reignited the furor that had surrounded Missouri's statehood petition during the previous Congress. For the next six weeks the Senate debated the expansion of slavery. Members who wanted to give new states the option of allowing slavery refused to approve Maine's bid for statehood unless Missouri's petition was also granted. Those who opposed the spread of slavery wanted to accept Maine into the Union and deal with Missouri as a separate issue.

Senator Jonathan Roberts of Pennsylvania argued that Maine's petition should be considered on its own merits. By linking the two bills, he said, the Senate had followed "an extraordinary mode of proceeding." The two issues, he noted, were "totally distinct." Maine's case was straightforward: the district was part of the original colonies, had unquestioned boundaries, had already formed a constitution, and had won the consent of the commonwealth from which it sought to be separated. Roberts cited "many more doubts" about Missouri's petition: that territory's boundaries and population

Missouri-Maine Bills

House Version
two separate bills:
- (Bill 1) Allow Maine to become a free state

- (Bill 2) Allow Missouri to prepare for statehood provided no additional slaves be brought into the region

Senate Version
one bill with amendment:
- Allow Maine to become a free state
- (Amendment) Allow Missouri to prepare for statehood (no restrictions on slavery)
Whether or not to allow slavery was left to the citizens of Missouri, who were expected to vote in favor of it

Final Compromise
two bills:

(Bill 1) Maine Statehood
- Allow Maine to become a free state

(Bill 2) Missouri Statehood
- Allow Missouri to prepare for statehood (no restrictions on slavery), and
- Ban slavery in all territory originally part of the Louisiana Purchase and located above the 36° 30' north latitude line, and
- Require the return of fugitive slaves found in the territory to the rightful owners

Note: Congress later approved a follow-up bill to grant statehood to Missouri.

had yet to be submitted and its constitution and "other questions" (presumably the slavery issue) had not been settled.

Several senators said it was unfair to ask them to support a cause they believed to be wrong (allowing Missouri to become a state without restrictions on slavery there) in order to win approval for the Maine petition, which everyone agreed to be right.

Southern legislators, however, took a different view. Senator Smith of South Carolina noted that both petitions dealt with the same topic, statehood, and both had to be judged by the same standards under the Constitution.

The amendment posed difficulties for Maine. In its resolution approving the district's independence, the Massachusetts legislature decreed that Maine had until March 4, 1820, to win Congress's approval for statehood. If it did not meet the deadline, Maine would remain under Massachusetts's jurisdiction. Mainers feared that the battle over extending slavery into Missouri would delay the vote and cost them the chance to form an independent state.

That circumstance did not sway southern senators. The fact that "the people of Maine had not foresight enough to take sufficient time" for their petition to be processed by Congress did not require lawmakers "to be hurried into the discussion of an important Constitutional question," Senator Edward Lloyd of Maryland noted. He argued that both states should be treated equally and as part of the same bill, or neither should be admitted to the Union. "Unless we can obtain the admission of Missouri into the Union, on the same terms and as free [to decide the slavery question on its own] and unshackled as Maine, I am decidedly of opinion we ought to admit neither," he said.

The discussion became more menacing as the debate

entered its second week. Senator James Barbour of Virginia warned that Missourians might rebel if their petition for statehood were denied. "The same spirit which animated the heroes and patriots of the Revolution warms the bosoms of those hardy sons of the West," he said. To continue to subjugate the residents of Missouri, he said, would be like trying to "arrest the mighty flood of the Mississippi." He feared that if the Senate rejected Missouri's petition to become a state, it would "be an ignited spark, which . . . will produce an explosion that will shake this Union to its centre."

Senator Samuel W. Dana, a Federalist from Connecticut, noted that never in the history of the nation had two states been admitted under a single bill. Nevertheless, the Senate voted by a 25 to 18 margin against separating the measures.

BITTER SENATE DEBATE

The following Monday, January 17, 1820, the Senate began the lengthy and increasingly bitter debate over admitting Maine and Missouri into the Union. In the weeks that followed, senators struggled to answer two questions:

- Does the U.S. Constitution grant Congress the power to place restrictions on prospective states?
- If so, can Congress, for the good of the nation, bar the introduction of new slaves in those states?

Most senators agreed that Congress could place some restrictions on regions applying for statehood. Southerners held that new states should be required to follow only the rules imposed on the original thirteen states. Those rules did not include restrictions on slavery. Northerners pointed out that the Constitution gave Congress the authority to accept or reject the applications of prospective states. As part of that process, they argued, Congress could impose certain requirements, including a ban on slavery. Both sides saw the issue as a serious matter, one that could split the nation in two if not resolved.

Southern senators argued for the right of self-government for all states, including those not yet admitted to the Union. "One-half of the States in the Union allow [slavery], and the Federal Constitution expressly recognises and sanctions it," John Elliott, Republican from Georgia, noted. "Under the Constitution, then, any State in this Union may admit involuntary servitude within its limits, in the exercise of its unquestionable right of self-government." To treat Missouri differently from Georgia, Virginia, or the other slave-holding states, he said, would "sow the seeds of jealousy and distrust" and ultimately would dissolve the Union.

Northern senators, too, used national unity to bolster their point of view. Senator David Morril of New Hampshire contended that the unrestricted extension of slavery into the new territories would impair the "stamina, nerve, muscle, and hope of the nation." States would pass opposing laws that would lead to discord and "the ruin of a country." He quoted Patrick Henry's words, spoken in 1799 in opposition to legislation that sought to give states the right to override laws passed by Congress, "United we stand—divided we fall."

FIRST COMPROMISE PROPOSAL

While the debate raged in Congress, President James Monroe, facing a reelection campaign in 1820, took no public stand on the matter. The controversy over the national bank and the economic panic of 1819 had weakened Monroe's power base in his home state of Virginia and in the rest of the South. Nevertheless, the president played a strong role in the drama, according to historian Robert Pierce Forbes. He saw the threat posed to a strong national government by opponents of federal bans on slavery. Monroe understood that his remaining southern supporters would turn against him if he made any move that favored legislators who were against slavery in Missouri. However, taking a proslavery stance would lose him the northern support he needed to fund roads and canals and other federal projects he wanted to accomplish.

Rather than making his opinion known, Monroe worked behind the scenes to win support for a compromise. Monroe's son-in-law, George Hay, wrote letters to Virginia newspapers opposing restrictions on slavery, while Monroe's ally in Congress, Senator James Barbour, proposed linking Maine's bid for statehood to that of Missouri. At the same time the president worked to put a compromise in place. Early in January 1820 Monroe wrote to Hay detailing a compromise that would set a boundary dividing free states and slave states.

On January 18, Senator Jesse B. Thomas, a Democratic Republican from Illinois, submitted a bill that would eventually serve as the basis for the Missouri Compromise. The bill called for extending the ban on slavery in the Northwest Ordinance to all the western territories that lay north of the 36° 30′ parallel, the same dividing line John Taylor of New York had proposed a year earlier in the House of Representatives. The proposed boundary line between slave territory and free territory ran along Missouri's southern border. Thomas's bill decreed that the 1787 ordinance should have "full force and effect in and over all the territory belonging to the United States" west of the Mississippi River and north of the line. No action was taken on the bill that day, and the Senate resumed the debate over Maine and Missouri.

During the ongoing debate Senator Freeman Walker of Georgia talked of "a storm portending" and foretold, with eerie accuracy, a civil war with "the father armed against the son" and "a brother's sword crimsoned with a brother's blood," with "houses wrapt in flames" and "wives and infant children driven from their homes."

Senator Prentiss Mellen, a Federalist from Massachusetts, dismissed the warnings. "I have better hopes and brighter views," he told his fellow legislators. "The bands which unite us are not so easily to be broken; we are a great, prosperous, and happy people."

POWER AND THE WEST EXPANSION

In addition to the dispute over slavery, the Maine-Missouri debate put the spotlight on the power struggle developing between the industry-rich North and the agricultural South. Beginning in the late 1700s the Industrial Revolution trans- formed northern cities and towns into centers of industry. Northern manufacturing interests quickly gained in influ- ence, enriching that region of the country and affecting the economy nationwide. The region's population soared as workers migrated north to work in the mills and other industries rapidly developed throughout the area.

Meanwhile, the cotton gin had made cotton the South's main crop. Cotton required large tracts of land. Southern planters came to rely even more heavily on the work of slaves to culti- vate the crop and prepare it for processing in manufacturing plants in the North. While the slave population grew, the num- ber of whites in the region decreased as planters expanded their landholdings to increase their cotton plantings.

The economy of the South depended on cotton, and the processing of cotton depended on slaves.

The imbalance in population growth gave the North more power in the House of Representatives, where each state's allotment of members was based on its number of residents. Even counting slaves as three-fifths of a white man, slave states had 76 seats in the House of Representatives versus the 104 seats held by free states in 1819, when the Maine-Missouri question surfaced. That gave free states much more clout than slave states in the House, unlike the Senate, where members from free states and slave states were evenly divided.

The move west to settle the lands acquired through the Louisiana Purchase and beyond also played into the battle for power and wealth among regions of the country. North-erners had mixed reactions to the migration. Some north-ern businessmen helped finance western development and benefited from the new settlements. Others feared that the West's pull would lure workers away from northern jobs and threaten the supply of cheap labor. The population growth in the West also threatened to dilute the power of both the South and the North.

Representative Henry Clay and several other congressmen from free states saluted the development of the vast lands that stretched to the West Coast. They saw the restrictions on slavery in Missouri as a roadblock to Americans' push westward. Senator Ninian Edwards, a Republican from Illi-nois, a state that barred slavery, noted that western devel-opment benefited the nation as a whole. The movement of slaves from the South to the West, he contended, would not increase the power of the South in the House of Represen-tatives. It would merely shift the number of representatives from southern to western states. The West, he said, had plenty of room for those who did not want to settle in areas that tolerated slavery.

LITTLE PROGRESS MADE

A month into the session, the debate over slavery and the admission of Maine and Missouri continued to rage. Some senators used a reasoned approach and presented a care-ful examination of the Constitution and other documents to prove their points. Others resorted to fiery rhetoric to push their view of the situation. Little progress appeared to have been made as senator after senator repeated the same argu-ments. Despite promises to be brief, few speakers were.

The Senate returned to the Missouri debate on January 20.

Arguments continued to center on whether Congress could or should ban slavery as a condition of statehood. Pennsylvania senator Walter Lowrie argued that Congress had every right to set requirements for prospective states, even if the original states did not have to meet such terms. "In the nine new States," Lowrie noted, "there are seventeen distinct conditions attached [as requirements to becoming a state], not one of which is applied to the old thirteen States." The conditions dealt with a number of issues, including taxation, waterways, and—as in Missouri—slavery.

Lowrie also argued that Missouri did not need new slaves in order to survive. On the other hand, he noted, a migration of slaves to the wide-open spaces of Missouri and regions to the west would make it even more difficult to eradicate slavery.

Senator Lowrie acknowledged that the nation was "drawing towards a very serious crisis" and warned that "all the wisdom of the present Congress" would be needed to resolve it. When faced with a choice between dissolving the Union and allowing the extension of slavery, however, Lowrie opted for the first. "The choice is a dreadful one," he told listeners. "Either side of the alternative fills my mind with horror." Lowrie ended on a more optimistic note, saying that he still believed the issue could be dealt with in a way that would satisfy the people of the United States.

Senator Nathaniel Macon of North Carolina warned that if the Union did dissolve over the issue, it would be far more difficult to form a new nation. He urged members to keep divisive political parties out of Congress, where they would "disturb and distract the Union." He echoed the sentiments of other southerners in describing the good treatment of slaves in the South and the difficulties involved if they were to be freed. If emancipation was so easy and so admirable, Macon asked, why had not the most prominent leaders in the nation—George Washington, Thomas Jefferson, Patrick Henry, and others—freed their own slaves? Arguing that slaveholders should be allowed to carry their property (slaves) into the new territory, Macon said that if the ban were upheld, it "may ruin us and our children after us." If, on the other hand, senators rejected the ban, "no injury will result to any part of the United States."

On January 21, Senator Thomas's compromise bill—to allow slavery in Missouri and areas to the south and to bar slavery to the north and west of Missouri—was sent to committee for review. The Senate reconvened on January 24, and Senator William Pinkney of Maryland spoke for several hours against a ban on slavery. A brilliant lawyer, Pinkney had successfully defended the federal bank in the landmark U.S. Supreme Court case *McCulloch* v. *Maryland*. In that case Pinkney had presented an eloquent argument supporting the supremacy of the federal government over individual states. In this debate, however, he spoke for states' rights, contending that states, not Congress, had the power to determine whether or not to tolerate slavery. Pinkney told the Senate that Congress could vote to accept or reject a petition for statehood. But, he continued, Congress did not have the power to restrict or limit the power of the state as a condition of admission to the Union.

With a touch of irony Senator Harrison Gray Otis of Massachusetts relied on Pinkney's own arguments from *McCulloch* to bolster the view that Congress had the power to impose conditions on states. He also debunked the South's contention that Missouri would be inferior to other states if the ban on slavery were approved. Ohio, Illinois, and Indiana all had

Senator William Pinkney of Maryland spoke fervently in favor of maintaining slavery throughout the United States.

joined the Union under a similar ban. Certainly none of them believed their states were "degraded" or "shorn of the rights of freedom and independence," Otis said.

Delaware's senator, Nicholas Van Dyke, parted ways with his state's legislature, which supported the slavery ban. He argued that the Declaration of Independence was never meant to cover slaves. While individual states had passed laws to free slaves within their borders, the nation had never done so. Under the Constitution, he pointed out, the federal government (Congress) did not have unlimited power, because states retained the powers not specifically granted to the federal government. "The proposed restriction," he argued, "is a direct invasion of the sovereignty of the State." If Congress denied Missouri the right to decide the slavery question for itself, he warned, it would set a dangerous precedent for future congresses tempted to take over other state powers.

Speakers droned on for hours at a time. Senator Barbour, in one of his many appearances on the floor, talked for more than three hours and had to postpone the remainder of his remarks when the Senate adjourned for the day. Members talked of war, hurled epithets at each other, and questioned opponents' sanity, humanity, morals, and religious beliefs. Northerners claimed that the U.S. policy toward slavery was a "blot on the national character" that degraded America's standing in the world. Southerners attacked such sentiments as unpatriotic and countered that other nations had their own flaws.

On February 1 senators killed another proposed amendment that would have restricted slavery in Missouri by a vote of 27 to 16. Only northerners supported the measure; southerners and several northern senators voted against it.

CHAPTER FOUR

Forging a Compromise

While many senators continued to take hard-line positions for or against the extension of slavery, several others began to talk of a compromise. Senator James Burrill Jr. noted that the Constitution itself was, "in great part, the fruit of compromise." Senator Harrison Gray Otis, who had voted for Missouri's first bid to become a state, said he would be willing to repeat his vote without the accompanying amendment banning slavery. In exchange, the Massachusetts lawmaker asked for assurances that slavery would be allowed to spread no farther west than Missouri.

On February 7, 1820, the Senate began debate on the compromise amendment proposed by Senator Jesse B. Thomas. The Judiciary Committee had reviewed the amendment and proposed that it be attached to the Maine–Missouri bill. A month later the proposal, almost word for word, would become Section 8 of the final version of the Missouri Compromise. The slavery issue would remain unsettled.

Thomas's amendment addressed two issues:
1. It banned slavery in all U.S. lands west of the Mississippi and north of 36° 30′ north latitude, with the exception of Missouri.
2. It required the return of fugitive slaves to their owners.

The amendment offered an incentive to the North—a ban on slavery in the northern territories (and future states)—and two incentives to the South—no restrictions on slavery in Missouri and a fugitive slave law.

STILL AT ODDS

Advocates on both sides of the issue hoped the amendment would help end the controversy at last. Other senators, however, vowed to continue the fight. Senator Rufus King of New York, one of the signers of the Constitution, based much of his argument against the amendment on his interpretation of the Declaration of Independence, the Constitution, and the 1787 Northwest Ordinance. An abolitionist and a passionate speaker, King outlined his case before a packed Senate chamber, which included freed slaves, among others, in the gallery. King concluded that any law that enslaved people was "absolutely void" because slavery was "contrary to the law of nature, which is the law of God."

After several postponements the debate on Thomas's amendment resumed on February 14. King's sharp criticism of slavery did not sit well with many of the senators, particularly those from the South. South Carolina's William Smith bristled at King's apparent unwillingness to compromise. The southern senator spent most of the following Monday disputing King's points and criticizing him for glorifying "the

Senator Rufus King of New York was a staunch opponent of slavery and a fierce voice in the debate.

Why Not the Women?

If a republic demanded that everyone—including black men—have equal rights, why not allow women to vote? One of the Senate's premier orators, William Pinkney of Maryland, attempted to shoot down the abolitionists' demands for a "purely republican government" by suggesting that such a system also apply to women. If Congress were to follow the "Utopian plan" proposed by the abolitionists, Pinkney noted, "and if it be true that all the men in a republican Government must help to wield its power, and be equal in rights, . . . why not all the women?" If abolitionists succeeded in giving slaves equal rights, he said he would not be surprised to find "some romantic reformer" proposing that women, too, be given "a full participation in political power."

There is no record of the senators' response to Pinkney's remarks, but it is likely that many of the senators chuckled at the outlandish notion of allowing women to vote and participate in government. Neither the House nor the Senate took Pinkney's suggestion as a serious proposal. White women were considered citizens, but as Representative Charles Pinckney of South Carolina noted, "their privileges vary according to their sex and situation. Females are wholly excluded from a right to vote, or to office, and are confined to their proper sphere."

Throughout the 1800s women had few civil rights under the law. Husbands or fathers controlled how money was spent, even if wives or daughters inherited it or earned it. In most states a woman could not sue or be sued, could not buy or sell property without her husband's permission, and could not even serve as legal guardian of her children. Few had much formal education. The first free high school for girls would not open until 1821, the year after Pinkney delivered his speech. Women would not gain the right to vote until 1920, long after the Fifteenth Amendment guaranteed freed male slaves voting rights in 1870.

religion of nature." He dismissed King's vision of abolishing slavery. "No human efforts can ever abolish slavery," Smith declared. "They may vary its form, but can never terminate it. . . . There has not been a period since the flood in which slavery did not prevail in every country known to man."

Senator William Pinkney jumped into the fray. Even after hearing the strong views expressed previously on the issue, Pinkney confessed that King's harshness had filled him with "astonishment."

The attempt to impose a ban on slavery in Missouri was strictly a power play by northern abolitionists, according to Pinkney. He charged that the ban's proponents disguised their attempt to take control by arguing for the ban in the name of "pity [for the slaves], of religion, of national honor, and national prosperity." He said any attempt to eliminate slavery would destroy the South. Freeing the slaves would require "a trespass of no ordinary kind—not the comparatively innocent trespass that beats down a few blades of grass which the first kind sun or the next refreshing shower may cause to spring again—but that which levels with the ground the lordliest trees of the forest, and claims immortality for the destruction which it inflicts."

He warned that other grabs for power would follow. "This," he said, "is the first inroad." Pinkney continued to hope, however, that the Missouri controversy could be settled "by some conciliatory compromise" that could reconcile the extreme views held by both sides.

REMARKABLE RESOLUTION

Meanwhile, in the House, New York Representative Henry Meigs introduced a remarkable proposal that revealed the commitment of some northerners to do away with slavery in the United States. In his remarks Meigs described slavery as "an evil of great and increasing magnitude; one which merits the greatest efforts of this nation to remedy." The resolution, read on February 5, 1820, called for a three-step plan of action to eradicate slavery:

1. Empower the navy to annihilate the slave trade.
2. Free all U.S. slaves.
3. Send the freed slaves to colonies in Africa, which would provide for their "comfort and happiness."

The House immediately tabled the proposal, where it languished without further action. However, the resolution sent a clear message to the South that forces in the nation fiercely opposed slavery and would do whatever they could to eliminate it. It further strengthened southerners' resolve against a federal government that would be powerful enough to carry out such proposals.

On February 16 the Senate voted to join the Maine and Missouri questions into one bill, reconfirming the earlier vote on the issue. The next day Thomas's amendment won initial approval from a majority of the Senate in a lopsided vote, 34 to 10. In a final vote that day, after the amendment had been tweaked to make the language uniform, another vote of the Senate endorsed the measure 24 to 20. After weeks of grueling debate, the Senate was ready at last to send the bill back to the House for its approval.

BACK TO THE HOUSE

The House received notice on February 18 that the Senate had approved the Maine bill along with the Missouri statehood amendment and Senator Thomas's compromise amendment. The House was still considering a bill to allow Missouri to take the initial steps toward statehood. This had not been linked to the Maine bill, as it had been in the Senate.

Initially the representatives rejected both amendments from the Senate. Several spoke against what they saw as an attempt to force them into taking quick action on the Missouri question by holding Maine's statehood hostage. Speaker of the House Henry Clay steered northerners away from attacks on the integrity of the Senate and, in stern tones, warned them not to impose their "New England notions" on the House. His warning, however, did little good.

Maine's request for statehood was the only portion of the bill approved by the House during the first round of votes. On February 23 the representatives voted 93 to 72 to separate the bill into two sections: one dealing with Missouri's request to prepare for statehood and one dealing with Maine's petition to become a state. The House then rejected the Missouri section 102 to 68, and the accompanying Thomas amendment by an even larger margin of 159 to 18.

For the next two days the House discussed the Missouri question and whether the spread of slavery could or should be restricted. John Scott, Missouri's nonvoting representative in the House, appealed to Congress not to restrict slavery in the state. Missouri's "present prosperity and future greatness depended on [Congress's] decision," he told the members of the House. After several more speeches for and against the amendment, the weary members looked for ways to stop the debate. As 5 p.m. approached, the representatives once again voted to ban slavery in Missouri, with a winning margin of a dozen or so votes. The House then adjourned for the day.

The following day, a Saturday, New York representative

Henry R. Storrs made a motion to insert wording very similar to that approved by the Senate, setting the 36° 30′ north
latitude as the boundary between slave territory and free
territory and allowing slavery in Missouri. Representative
John Randolph of Virginia, who opposed any restriction on
slavery, spoke at length against the proposal.

On Monday, February 28, as the House considered other
matters, the Senate sent word that that body would *insist* on
its amendments to the Maine-Missouri statehood bill. Representative John W. Taylor immediately moved that the House
insist on its own version as well, and a majority of the members voted for his motion. After the clerk informed the Senate of the House's decision to remain firm on its version of
the bill, the two bodies agreed to hold a joint conference to
discuss the matter. Meanwhile, the House continued its discussion of the bill to admit Missouri as a state and Storrs's
amendment to ban slavery in the northern portion of the
territory. Despite Speaker Clay's strenuous attempts to pass
a bill resembling the compromise measure agreed to in the
Senate, House members voted against the Storrs amendment.

A STANDOFF

The following day, February 29, as Maine's deadline loomed
near, the full House prepared to take a final look at the Missouri bill. Representative Thomas Forrest pulled out all
the stops in urging House members not to support a compromise measure that allowed the extension of slavery. He
served up images of George Washington as the general urged
on young American patriots at the Battle of Trenton. Forrest
spoke of his memories of a war in which soldiers had to cut
up their blankets to outfit themselves. His fellow patriots
had sacrificed their lives for posterity, Forrest reminded the

House members. It filled him with sadness, he said, that their deaths had ensured a posterity that now was considering an extension of slavery. And he expressed sorrow that members had been reduced to using "denunciation, sarcasm, and insinuation" in their debates over the issue.

Later that day the House voted again to restrict slavery in Missouri, this time by a margin of 94 to 86. Representatives then voted 93 to 84 to allow Missouri to prepare for statehood on the condition that no additional slaves be brought within its borders.

The House learned the next day of the death of Representative David Walker of Kentucky, who had opposed restrictions on slavery during the session. Following the congressman's last request, the House did not adjourn for the day—the common practice when a member died—and instead continued with the Missouri vote. Randolph, who had asked for an adjournment in vain, argued for more than three hours against the bill's "unconstitutional and unjust restriction . . . imposed on the people of Missouri." Unswayed by the Virginian's furious words, members approved the third reading of the bill on a vote of 91 to 82 and sent it to the Senate for its concurrence.

It did not take the Senate long to act on the bill. After first removing the House antislavery amendment from the Missouri bill, senators voted to reattach the compromise amendment proposed by Senator Thomas and Representative Storrs. The Senate then approved the Missouri bill with the compromise amendment and referred it back to the House.

"AN AWFUL RESPONSIBILITY"

On March 2 several House members tried unsuccessfully to open hearings on various appropriations bills that had been delayed during the Missouri debate. Speaker Clay urged the members to postpone consideration of the spending bills. Until the Missouri bill had been settled, he told the House, he, "for one, was unwilling to go into any other important business." Clay made it clear that he was weary of the affair and wished the bill "to be first finally disposed of" and then "wanted a day's rest for the body as well as the mind, after the settlement of this agitating and laborious subject."

The joint House-Senate conference, meanwhile, had completed its negotiations and had come out in favor of the compromise proposed by Thomas and Storrs. Representative John Holmes of Massachusetts presented the conference report, which proposed two bills, one to make Maine a state and one to allow Missouri to prepare for statehood with no restrictions on slavery. The second bill also banned slavery north of the 36° 30′ line. Benjamin Adams, representative from Massachusetts, spoke "at length" against the compromise, but several others urged its passage to "restore tranquility to the country."

While antislavery northerners did not like the compromise amendment, the fiercest opposition came from Representative Randolph of Virginia and other southerners. They saw the issue as a fight to protect their property and their survival. The compromise, as they saw it, ceded state power to a federal government strong enough to eliminate slavery altogether if it desired.

Backers of the compromise used a number of tactics to persuade balking congressmen to vote for the proposal. They promoted the theory that the Federalists had devised the whole Missouri question as a scheme to split the Democratic-Republicans into North-South factions and allow Federalist Rufus King to capture the presidency. If the matter was not settled quickly, they argued, it would weaken the Monroe administration and open the door to a Federalist takeover. Democratic-Republicans in the North hated Federalists as much as southerners did. For his part, President James Monroe used all the tools available to him to turn the tide for compromise, according to historian Robert Pierce Forbes. Monroe made job offers, promised political support and patronage, called on Thomas Jefferson and business allies for support, and used his influence in other ways to convince Congress to pass the bill.

The long debate had stalled important matters in Congress and had sparked sectional hostilities. Some truly believed a stalemate would threaten the continued existence of the United States as one nation. Many representatives simply reached the end of their patience over the whole affair. Members of the House had been forced to sit and listen to the debates for weeks on end, fearing that if they left the chamber, they would miss the vote on the issue. Massachusetts congressmen, several of whom lived in the District of Maine, faced the additional pressure of the upcoming deadline for the district's bid for statehood.

Representative Charles Kinsey of New Jersey became the first to change his position from opposing the compromise to agreeing to it. The northern manufacturer needed southern support for protective tariffs that would give his business an edge over cheaper imports. Explaining his change of heart, he said the prospect that the nation would dissolve over the dispute "presents itself in all the horrid, gloomy features of reality." He noted that he had voted over the past six weeks with the majority of the House to restrict slavery in Missouri. But, he said, "should we persist to reject the olive branch now offered [by the Senate], the most disastrous consequences will follow." Noting that the South had agreed to a boundary that barred slavery in nine-tenths of the lands obtained through the Louisiana Purchase, Kinsey asked whether members could justify opposing such a "reasonable . . . proposition." He suggested that opponents of the compromise might be taking the stance to win political advantage over the South. Acknowledging that his constituents might not agree with his decision, Kinsey nevertheless said he would vote for the compromise for the good of the nation. "An awful responsibility rests upon us," he declared.

Representative James Stevens of Connecticut, who like Kinsey had opposed the measure, rose to add his voice to those reversing their stand. Just as the founders forged the Constitution in the spirit of compromise, Stevens said, so should the present Congress be willing to make sacrifices for the general good. Though he feared that the compromise's boundary line would divide the North and South into separate political parties, Stevens called for Congress to pass the compromise. To do otherwise, he said, would "create ruthless hatred, irradicable jealousy, and a total forgetfulness of the ardor of patriotism."

AGREEMENT AT LAST

After almost six weeks of bitter and heated debate on the matter, the House voted 90 to 87 to allow Missouri to seek statehood without the ban on slavery. Congressmen Samuel Eddy of Rhode Island and Bernard Smith of New Jersey joined fellow representatives Kinsey and Stevens on the side of the majority. Three other northern legislators—Walter Case and Caleb Tompkins of New York and Henry Edwards of Connecticut—did not vote. In all, seventeen congressmen from free states voted with representatives from slave states in approving the measure. The vote was the first step in adopting the entire compromise package.

A much wider margin, 134 to 42, approved the compromise amendment banning slavery north of the 36° 30′ line. Representative Randolph voted with the majority to lift the ban on Missouri, but he, along with several other diehard southerners, sided with the northern holdouts in voting against the amendment. Randolph, who opposed the compromise because he wanted no restrictions on slavery, tried to delay the bill by asking the House to reconsider it, but his attempts failed. Furious, he mocked the antislavery northerners who had reversed their vote on the issue and called them "doughfaces" for compromising their principles. On March 3, 1820, with only hours to spare before the Maine deadline, the House and the Senate approved the final part of the compromise—the admission of Maine into the Union.

The compromise pleased neither side but granted something to both. Missouri would join the Union as a slave state, and Arkansas would follow. Slavery would be banned in the rest of the Louisiana Purchase territory that lay north of the 36° 30′ line of latitude. This included the future states of Minnesota, Kansas, Nebraska, and Iowa. At the time most of the territory that fell under the antislavery ban was unsettled wilderness.

The first seven sections of the Missouri act addressed the formation of the state of Missouri, its boundaries, the operation of its government, and the rights of its citizens. The territory, according to the act, would be "admitted into the Union, upon an equal footing with the original states, in all respects whatsoever."

The eighth and last section dealt with the issue that had sparked the months-long debate in Congress: the extension of slavery into new U.S. territories. The section "forever pro-hibited" slavery in all lands gained through the Louisiana Purchase that lay north of 36° 30′ latitude. As a concession to the South, the new state of Missouri, which lay north of the boundary, would be permitted to have slaves within its borders. Section 8 also included the Fugitive Slave Act, a decree demanded by the South that required the return of slaves who escaped into free territory.

President James Monroe did not share his views publicly while Congress debated the issue, but he confided to Thomas Jefferson in a letter written on February 19, 1820, "I have never known a question so menacing to the tranquility and even the continuance of our Union as the present one." When the president received the bill for his signature, Monroe's cabinet members disagreed over whether the slavery ban applied to territories after they became states. Rather than delay the matter, the cabinet agreed to disagree and merely asserted that the measure was constitutional. Monroe signed the Missouri Compromise into law on March 6. Maine officially joined the Union as the twenty-third state on March 15, 1820.

CHAPTER FIVE

The Second Missouri Compromise

The dispute did not end with the signing of the Missouri Compromise. On July 1, 1820, Missouri, as expected, adopted a state constitution that allowed slavery. The state constitution also barred the Missouri legislature from freeing Missouri's slaves without first gaining the approval of the slaveholders—which effectively ensured that slavery would continue in the state. Under another provision the legislature could not pass laws to stop settlers from bringing slaves into Missouri as long as slavery was legal in the state. The most controversial provision barred free blacks from entering the state.

White residents of Missouri, like other southern slaveholders, feared the presence of free blacks in their communities. They worried that slaves might attempt the kind of rebellion that devastated Haiti in the 1790s and eventually led to the overthrow of white landowners and control of the island by the former slaves. Slaveholders believed that free blacks

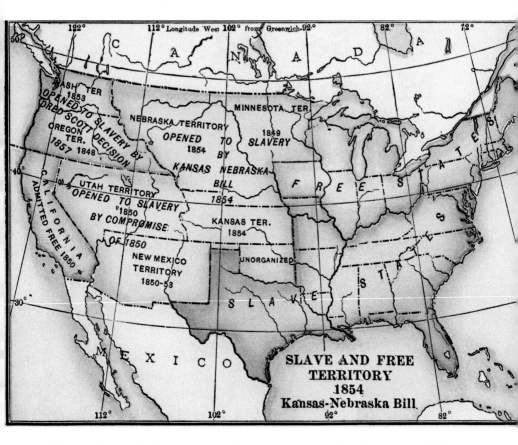

This map shows the free states and slave states set up with the passage of the Missouri Compromise.

might organize a rebellion or, at the least, inspire slaves to seek their own freedom.

Beginning in 1800 slaves in the United States staged several revolts. A young man known as Gabriel led the first major slave rebellion in Virginia in 1800. Trained as a blacksmith, he worked as a slave on a tobacco plantation in Henrico County, Virginia, owned by Thomas Prosser. Gabriel, who could read and write, began plotting a revolution in 1799. Inspired by the slave rebellion in Haiti, he gathered support from hundreds of slaves throughout central Virginia, as well as from free blacks and a few poor white laborers. He aimed to free the state's slaves and set up a society of equals. His well-planned scheme included taking control of Richmond, the capital of Virginia, and using Governor James Monroe as a hostage to win his demands.

On the day of the planned attack, August 30, 1800, floods ravaged the area and rendered the bridges and roads leading into Richmond impassable. Gabriel delayed the assault until the following day. By that time, however, word of the plot had leaked out. State militia rounded up about thirty of Gabriel's followers, some of whom testified against their leader in court. Gabriel was captured several days later, and he and more than two dozen other slaves were hanged. Owners of the executed slaves collected more than $8,900 from the state of Virginia to compensate them for their loss.

Although Gabriel failed, his well-planned rebellion and other slave revolts increased southerners' fears and led to Missouri's attempts to keep free blacks out of the state.

"CONFEDERACY OF KINDRED REPUBLICS"

The Missouri constitution, in particular its exclusion of free blacks, enraged northerners, who threatened to block Missouri's admittance into the Union. Free blacks were considered citizens in several states in the North, and northerners argued that Missouri's attempts to prevent free blacks from entering its borders violated the U.S. Constitution's guarantee, in Article 4, that "citizens of each state shall be entitled to all privileges and immunities of citizens of the several states." As Senator James Burrill of Rhode Island would point out during the Senate debate on the matter, the states were "a confederacy of kindred republics." As such, under the Constitution, they were obligated to respect each other's laws.

The issue came before the Senate when the Sixteenth Congress assembled for its second session, on November 14, 1820. John Chandler and John Holmes took their seats as Maine senators for the first time. On its second day in session the Senate listened to the reading of the Missouri constitution, as required under the rules for admitting new states. The proposed constitution was then referred to committee, part of the procedure to be followed before Missouri could be accepted as a full-fledged state. State legislatures in both New York and Vermont submitted resolutions asking Congress not to accept Missouri's proslavery, antiblack constitution.

On November 29 the Senate committee that was reviewing Missouri's constitution submitted a resolution to admit Missouri as a state with its constitution intact. Several senators objected. As a compromise, Senator John Henry Eaton, a Democratic-Republican from Tennessee, proposed adding an amendment that Congress would not approve any provision that deprived citizens of their rights. Senator Rufus King and others objected that the amendment was not specific enough and should apply directly to the clause referring to the ban on free blacks. In a close vote of 24 to 21, the Senate voted against Eaton's amendment.

Senator Burrill of Rhode Island, a member of the committee who had voted against the resolution to admit Missouri with its current constitution, protested that the document was "repugnant to the Constitution of the United States. It prohibits a very large class of persons from entering the State at all." The clause barring free blacks, he said, ignored the agreement among states to honor each other's laws. "The States of this Union were not distinct and independent nations," Burrill stated. He said it would be easy for Missouri to win Congress's approval by holding another convention and revising its constitution so that it complied with the U.S. Constitution.

Senator William Smith of South Carolina, chair of the review committee, countered Senator Burrill's arguments with ones of his own. The drawing up of a constitution, he contended, should be left to each state. He spent the next few hours presenting in detail the constitutions of other states that had been accepted as "republican" despite passages that might be questioned. Likewise, Smith concluded, it was only fair to accept Missouri's constitution.

Senator Holmes, who had fought to give blacks the vote in Maine's constitution, nevertheless concurred with Smith, noting that to bar Missouri at this stage would "be against all precedent." The courts could decide whether the Missouri constitution contained flaws, he said.

On December 11 Senator Eaton resubmitted his amendment to the full Senate. This time the senators approved the measure, with 23 voting in favor of it. After further debate, the Senate finally approved Missouri's bid to join the Union on December 12, 1820. The resolution, with Eaton's amendment attached, passed on a vote of 26 to 18 and was sent to the House for its concurrence on the bill.

COMMITTEE'S RESOLUTION

Henry Clay had resigned as speaker of the House but continued to serve as a representative. John Taylor of New York had been elected to take his place. In February 1821 the House took up the bill to admit Missouri as a state. Missouri's defiant constitution reignited the controversy that had flared in the House during the previous two sessions. Clay resumed his role as peacemaker, heading a thirteen-member committee to settle the issue. For eight days the members worked on a resolution to soften the Missouri constitution. The committee's final report, in the form of an amendment, called for Missouri to pass a resolution before being admitted as a state. Missouri would be required to pledge that the state would "never pass any law preventing any description of persons from coming to or settling in the . . . state, who are now or may hereafter become citizens of any of the States of this Union."

Neither side liked the confusing amendment. The antislavery forces thought it was not specific enough and did little to offset the offending provision in the Missouri constitution. Proslavery and states' rights advocates believed Congress should put no more conditions on Missouri. Several Missouri citizens had already suggested they would form an independent nation if they were forced to change their constitution. The committee's amendment reopened the debate over slavery and states' rights and introduced a new controversy over whether free blacks could legitimately be considered U.S. citizens.

Antislavery advocates argued that Missouri should remove the offending sections from its constitution. Representative Gideon Tomlinson of Connecticut, a dissenting member of Clay's committee, said he could not admit a state "with a constitution containing a provision directly repugnant to [the U.S. Constitution] which I have sworn to support." Proslavery spokesmen argued that Missouri had the right to decide for itself what its constitution contained and who qualified as citizens in the state.

On February 12, after several close, contentious votes, the House approved the committee's proposed amendment but then rejected, 80 to 83, the bill to allow Missouri to join the Union. Among those voting against the Missouri bill (with the committee's amendment attached) was Virginia's John Randolph. He later argued that Congress should decide a petition for statehood without attaching any conditions whatsoever to it.

WHEN IS A CITIZEN NOT A CITIZEN?

The unsettled issue disrupted the work of the Electoral College, which met in February 1821 to affirm James Monroe's reelection as president. Monroe had run for president unopposed in November 1820. Since the Senate had approved Missouri's petition to become a state, some senators wanted to count the votes of Missouri's three electors. Opponents, noting that the House had rejected the Senate's bill, insisted that Missouri had not yet become a state, so its electoral votes should not be counted. The disagreement made no difference to the outcome of the election, since Monroe had the support of all but New Hampshire's elector, who cast his ballot for John Quincy Adams. However, the dispute heightened the tension over Missouri's statehood.

The day after rejecting Missouri's statehood bill, the House reconsidered the vote. During the ensuing debate Representative Charles Pinckney of South Carolina, one of the signers of the U.S. Constitution, argued that blacks had never been considered citizens under the U.S. Constitution. "Nor," he added, "do I now believe one [black citizen] does exist." He pointed out that free blacks in the North were denied many of the rights of white citizens, including the right to serve on juries, the right to live in certain areas, and the right to marry whites. That proved, as far as he was concerned, that blacks were not citizens, even in the North. He went on to describe Africans as "savage" and having been "created with less intellectual powers than the whites."

Pinckney also made note of the North's faltering economy and northern shippers' and manufacturers' reliance on the South and West for trade and raw materials. "In this state of things," he told the House, "it is almost superfluous to ask if it is not of much greater consequence to the Northern and Eastern States to preserve an Union from which they derive such very important benefits, than to risk it to give to a few free negroes and mulattoes the right to settle in Missouri contrary to the declared unanimous wish of the people of that State?"

Clay closed the main debate with a plea to the House to pass the bill with the committee's amendment. "He alternately reasoned, remonstrated, and entreated with the House to settle forever this agitating question, by passing the resolution before it," according to the recorder of the proceedings. Despite Clay's appeal the House once again rejected the bill on a close vote, with 82 favoring the measure and 88 opposed.

When the matter came up for discussion again on February 21, Representative William Brown of Kentucky submitted a resolution that aimed to dismantle the first Missouri Compromise. Calling on "the principles of eternal justice," he demanded that Congress lift the restrictions on slavery in the western territories passed during the previous session. He argued that Congress, in refusing to admit Missouri as a state, had not kept up its end of the bargain. The House voted against considering Brown's proposal by a wide margin, 79 to 43. But the threat to undo the work of the last session helped spur members to work out a solution. Those opposed to bans on slavery, in particular, wanted to settle the Missouri question before the seventeenth Congress was seated. They believed, rightly, that northern voters, angry

This symbolic group portrait eulogizes the Missouri Compromise, which was seen at the time as a way of preserving the Union. In later years the compromise was tossed aside, and the nation spiraled downward into a devastating civil war.

at members who voted with the South on the compromise, would replace them with stronger antislavery candidates.

RESOLVED—"FOR THE MOMENT"

The next day Clay made a motion to set up a joint committee of House and Senate members to resolve the matter. The result was a vaguely worded resolution that the committee issued the following Monday. It admitted Missouri as a state with the proviso that the disputed constitutional clause "shall never be construed to authorize the passage of any law . . . by which any citizen . . . of the States in this Union shall be excluded from the enjoyment of any of the privileges and immunities to which such citizen is entitled under the Constitution of the United States." Proponents of each side interpreted the language to mean what they wanted it to. It said nothing about the question of whether blacks could be U.S. citizens.

After some discussion, on February 26, 1821, a weary House approved the resolution 87 to 81. Two days later, the Senate, with no debate, voted 28 to 14 for the measure. On August 10, 1821, Missouri officially became the nation's twenty-fourth state, settling the Missouri question at last. The bitter controversy over slavery, however, would not be put to rest.

Two months after Congress forged the compromise, Thomas Jefferson wrote a friend that he believed the controversy had been "hushed . . . for the moment." But he held out little hope that the crisis between slave states and free states had been put to rest. "This is a reprieve only, not a final sentence. A geographical line, coinciding with a marked principle, moral and political, once conceived and held up to the angry passions of men, will never be obliterated; and every new irritation will mark it deeper and deeper."

Repeal of the Missouri Compromise

The passage of the Missouri Compromise seemed to quell the unrest over the slavery issue, at least temporarily. Newspapers in the North and the South hailed Henry Clay as the "Great Pacificator" for his efforts in winning the bill's approval. However, the compromise itself met with both criticism and praise from all parts of the country.

John Randolph, the congressman from Virginia who waged a bitter fight against any restriction on slavery, called it a "dirty bargain." An editorial in Virginia's *Richmond Enquirer* protested the passage of the bill: "We scarcely ever recollected to have tasted of a bitterer cup."

Representative Charles Pinckney of South Carolina, however, said the slave states of the South considered the compromise "a great triumph." Representative James Tallmadge, who had proposed the original amendment to restrict slavery in Missouri, and Representative John Taylor, who pushed for the amendment, both treated the final passage of the compromise as worthwhile, if not a win. "We have gained all that was possible ... an ample recompense for all the time and labour it has cost us," Taylor wrote to his wife.

On the whole, southerners—almost all of whom voted for the compromise—saw the deal as a victory, while northerners regarded it as a defeat. New York's Rufus King confided to his son that he considered himself "conquered" by the Missouri debate's outcome. The compromise, he said, "is a mere tub to the whale," and the free states had lost "the only opportunity ... to establish the equal rights of [their] citizens."

At least one prominent American leader of the time believed that Congress should have addressed the question of slavery once and for all instead of settling for a compromise. John Quincy Adams, secretary of state under President James Monroe and later president, said he favored the compromise, "believing it all that could be effected under the present Constitution."

But, he admitted, it might have been wiser to insist on a slavery ban in Missouri. He believed that course of action would have forced the states to hold a new constitutional convention to settle their differences. Under those circumstances, Adams said, northerners would have amended the Constitution to ban slavery and formed a new nation made up of "thirteen or fourteen States, unpolluted with slavery." This new union, according to Adams, would have set out to attract other states, which would have been allowed to join once they freed the slaves within their borders and banned slavery.

Since that had not happened, Adams said, slavery would be the question "on which [the Union] ought to break. For the present, however, this contest is laid asleep."

PAYING A PRICE

The few northern politicians who supported the compromise paid a price. Senator John F. Parrott of New Hampshire voted for the deal and later "dropped dead as a stone politically, and never recovered," according to an 1854 article in the New York *Tribune*. Senator William A. Palmer of Vermont suffered a similar fate, only to gain a following twenty years later as a member of the Anti-Masonic Party. Senator John Holmes of Maine and Representative Henry R. Storrs of New York "were temporarily crushed," the *Tribune* reported. Henry Shaw lost his seat as a House member from Massachusetts for supporting the compromise. "There can be no dispute," according to the *Tribune* article, "that the North considered that Compromise a betrayal of its rights and surrender of its principles, and discarded almost every public man who promoted it."

Politicians learned from the experience and avoided another prolonged discussion of slavery. For the next twenty-five years states joined the Union according to the restrictions laid out in the Missouri Compromise. Arkansas, which fell south of the line and allowed slavery, became a state in 1836. The following year Michigan, north of the line, joined the Union as a free state. Their slavery status aroused little debate. In 1845 Florida joined as a slave state. The same year Texas, for the most part south of the line, was admitted as a slave state, although slavery was forbidden in the sections that lay north of the boundary. Iowa and Wisconsin, both located north of the line, became free states in 1846 and 1848, respectively.

In 1849 Stephen A. Douglas, who would later become the slave states' advocate and Abraham Lincoln's opponent during the 1858 election for U.S. senator for Illinois, praised the Missouri Compromise as "that great patriotic measure" and likened its origins to that of the U.S. Constitution. At the time the compromise was approved, Douglas noted, it was "canonized in the hearts of the American people, as a sacred thing which no ruthless hand would ever be reckless enough to disturb." Douglas, of course, changed his views when he became a leader in the campaign for states' rights.

COMPROMISE OF 1850

The slavery issue surfaced again during the war over territory between the United States and Mexico, which raged from 1846 to 1848. In 1846 U.S. President James Polk asked Congress to allot $2 million to be used to negotiate a peace settlement with Mexico and to purchase some of the disputed territory. Representative David Wilmot, a Democrat from Pennsylvania, added an amendment to the original appropriations bill that banned slavery "in any territory thus acquired." As in the Missouri dispute, the Senate supported slavery for the most part, while the House of Representatives continued its efforts to stop the spread of slavery.

Despite considerable controversy over the Wilmot rider, the House approved the measure and voted for the amended version of the bill. The Senate, however, adjourned before taking final action, and the bill died. A similar scenario took place in Congress the following year, again rejecting the president's plea for funds.

Over the course of the war the antislavery proposal came to a vote more than forty times. Each time the Senate prevented it from becoming law. Ultimately, the United States and Mexico agreed to a treaty, signed in 1848, that gave the United States a large chunk of territory later encompassing the states of Arizona, New Mexico, and California, as well

The Compromise of 1850, allowing the admission of California as a free state, incited violent opposition in the Senate. This tongue-in-cheek cartoon depicts the infamous dispute between Senator Henry S. Foote of Mississippi, who supported the pact, and Senator Thomas Hart Benton of Missouri, who opposed it. In a rage, Benton shouted at Foote for his antislavery stand. Foote drew a pistol on Benton, supposedly to protect himself. President Fillmore called for order on the Senate floor, as visitors fled in panic. No one was injured in the incident, and the Senate eventually passed the new compromise.

as parts of Nevada, Utah, and Colorado. The treaty made no mention of slavery.

The antislavery forces pushed to allow the admittance of California as a free state. After the discovery of gold in 1848 brought thousands of fortune seekers to the territory, California petitioned to join the Union. In 1849, before being accepted as a state, California approved a constitution that barred slavery within its borders. As the largest segment of land gained through the settlement with Mexico, California's

population would add a considerable number of congressmen to the antislavery vote, once it achieved statehood.
Those in the Senate who opposed a ban on slavery, therefore,
refused to approve California's petition.

It took another compromise to settle the dispute. Henry
Clay, the architect of the earlier pact, also fashioned the new
one. The Compromise of 1850, written by Clay and pushed
through Congress by Senator Douglas and Senator Daniel
Webster, a Whig from Massachusetts, resembled the previous deal worked out three decades earlier. Again, Congress
agreed to it because lawmakers feared the Union would dissolve if they did not resolve the matter. The compromise gave
the South a much stronger fugitive slave law, which required
free states to return runaway slaves. Proslavery advocates
also won a concession that allowed the territories of Utah
and New Mexico to decide the status of slavery within their
own borders when they applied for statehood. The North got
California as a new free state and won a longstanding battle
to abolish the slave trade in the nation's capital. As part of
the compromise Texas received $10 million to pay off debts
in exchange for giving up claims to northwestern areas (and
thus limiting the northwestern boundary of slave states to
the new Texas line).

During an interview on February 10, 1850, with the *Richmond Enquirer*, Clay agreed that "it was necessary to settle
the whole subject at once and forever, in order to secure the
peace, the union, and the permanent prosperity of [the]
country."

A NEW "PANDORA'S BOX"
The Compromise of 1850 could not forestall for long the bitter dispute over slavery and its role in the new territories.

The political power wielded by the nation's 300,000 slave-holders, who owned three million slaves in half the states, was "startling," in the words of Representative J. W. Edmands of Massachusetts. They used their votes and their wealth to launch a campaign to open the Nebraska Territory to slavery. The region, about a third as large as the established states combined, lay north of the boundary set by the Missouri Compromise, in the area where slavery was specifically prohibited. As vast as the area was, few settlers had migrated to the region. Nevertheless, a call went up for the immediate organization of the territory. Many believed that the request came not from the settlers in Nebraska but from southern slaveholders, in particular settlers in Missouri who wanted to expand their landholdings into the territory.

The commissioner of Indian Affairs reported in November 1853 that no settlements existed "in any part of Nebraska" as of October of that year. "From all the information I could obtain," the report noted, "there were but three white men in the Territory, except such as were there by authority of law [soldiers], and those adopted by marriage and otherwise, into Indian families." Along the eastern border of the Nebraska territory, in the western counties of Missouri, nearly 80,000 white settlers lived with 12,000 slaves. The entire state of Missouri contained a population of nearly 600,000 whites and more than 87,000 slaves.

In 1853 the House of Representatives passed a bill granting Nebraska a territorial government and leaving the ban on slavery unchanged. The bill died when the Senate failed to act on it. The following year Senator Douglas introduced a similar bill, but a month after introducing it, he added an amendment that would allow residents to bring slaves to the region. If approved, this measure would repeal the Missouri

Henry Clay:
The Man Who Held

Like many of America's founders, Henry Clay was a Virginian. He was born near Richmond—the heart of the South—in 1777, a year after the start of the Revolutionary War. The noted statesman considered himself a citizen of the nation. After being chastised for not siding with the South during an 1850 debate over California's statehood petition, Clay declared to his fellow senators, "I know no South, no North, no East, no West to which I owe any allegiance. My allegiance is to this American Union and to my own State."

As a young man Clay migrated to Kentucky, where he opened a law practice. Elected to fill a vacancy in Kentucky's delegation to the U.S. Senate, he held the post from November 1806 to March 1807, even though at twenty-nine, he was five months shy of the age required by the U.S. Constitution. Because of his popularity and the overwhelming support of Kentucky leaders, the Senate overlooked this issue. He again filled a Senate vacancy in 1810.

From then until his death in 1852, Clay continually served as a public official in a variety of posts, including speaker of the House of Representatives in six Congresses, secretary of state, and three-time unsuccessful candidate for U.S. president. A dynamic speaker and a master of the art of persuasion, he won fame as chief negotiator in the battle to pass the Missouri Compromise and the eventual acceptance of Missouri as a state. He repeated the role in molding the Compromise of 1850, which divided western lands into slave territory and free territory. These achievements earned Clay the nicknames "The Great Compromiser" and "The Great Pacificator." Historians have called him the man who held the Union together.

Clay's ability to bring both sides together in the slavery

debate served the nation well by postponing the Civil War. His role as "compromiser," however, played a role in his doomed run for president, the political post he most wanted. Enemies on both sides of the issue worked against him. Andrew Jackson, his bitterest enemy, won an overwhelming victory over Clay in the presidential race of 1832. He also lost in 1824 and 1844.

Clay was a man of opposites, a slaveholder who detested slavery; a peacemaker with a volatile temper who participated in two duels, one with Virginia Senator John Randolph. (The duel ended with a handshake after Clay, then secretary of state, shot a hole in Randolph's coat.) Clay was a farmer, noted for first bringing Hereford cattle to the United States, who spent much of his time in the city crafting laws; an ambitious, arrogant party politician who used his considerable skill in diplomacy to forge nonpartisan agreements. He relied on slave labor to operate his farm in Kentucky, yet as president of the American Colonization Society, he worked to accomplish its goal of emancipating slaves and sending them to colonies set up for them in Africa.

Even in the midst of his failed presidential campaigns, Clay devoted his political career to preserving the Union. Unlike many of his southern neighbors Clay believed in a strong central government with the power to hold together the various sections of the country—with their different, and often competing, interests. "It has been my invariable rule to do all for the Union," he said in a speech in Norfolk, Virginia, during his ill-fated presidential campaign in 1844. "If any man wants the key to my heart, let him take the key of the Union, and that is the key to my heart."

Compromise and its ban on slavery in the northern territories. Under Douglas's proposal the citizens living in the territory could decide for themselves whether or not to allow slavery within their borders. Another proposed amendment divided the territory in two. The southern section would become Kansas; the northern parcel, Nebraska.

Opposition to Douglas's Kansas-Nebraska Act was fierce in the North and much of the Northwest. The South, for the most part, supported the measure. Southern slaveholders rallied behind any legislation that upheld the right to own slaves. They also stood to gain financially from an extension of slavery into the Northwest. An article published in the *New York Times* on May 13, 1854, estimated that the introduction of slavery into the Nebraska Territory would up the demand for slaves and thus increase the value of each slave held by southern plantation owners by 5 percent.

Several southern senators testifying in favor of the bill insisted that Nebraska and Kansas would not be slaveholding states. Northerners, however, questioned their sincerity. If that were the case, they argued, why did southerners oppose the bill to organize the territory under the terms of the Missouri Compromise but support a similar bill that allowed slavery in the region?

Supporters of the bill claimed that Section 8 of the Missouri Compromise, which set the boundary between slave territory and free territory, was "inconsistent with the principle of non-intervention by Congress with slavery in the States and Territories." The Nebraska-Kansas law, they said, would right the wrongs of the earlier compromise by not interfering in a state's affairs and not discriminating against regions that preferred to allow slavery within their borders. The bill's proponents argued that the nation should follow the dictates of the more recent Compromise of 1850, which had allowed residents in the newly established states of Texas and California and in the Utah and New Mexico territories to determine for themselves whether to allow slavery. The 1850 law, southerners contended, should apply to all future states and organized territories. Southerners also protested that it was unfair to allow northerners to transport their possessions to the northwest regions but to bar southern plantation owners from bringing their slaves, whom they considered their property, into the area.

Congressmen delivered many of the same arguments used during the Missouri controversy. In the House, Representative Alfred H. Colquitt of Georgia urged his fellow legislators to "throw open the portals to the mighty West, and invite master and slave into her fruitful and teeming valleys." Lifting the restrictions on slavery in the western territory would benefit slaveholders and slaves, the community and the country, Colquitt contended. If slavery were allowed in the western lands, he argued, slaves would be "dispersed rather than crowded together and confined to one locality." The alternative, he noted, would be to "build a wall of fire around slavery." Unlike the Missouri Compromise ban, the new laws would not "invade the sanctuary of the States," he said.

According to the census of 1850, slave states occupied 928,947 square miles, while free states occupied 643,326 square miles. Northern states, however, held the advantage when it came to population. Slave states had 9,663,997 residents, including 3 million slaves. Nearly 13.5 million people resided in free states.

The majority of newspapers in the Northwest strenuously opposed Douglas's Nebraska bill. "The more this Nebraska question is discussed, the more unanimous must the

Democracy become that Judge [Stephen] Douglas has made a sad mistake," commented an editorial writer in the *Democratic Press* of Chicago. Whig journals renounced the bill "as a proposal of personal dishonor," according to a report in the *New York Times*. Douglas, as author of the bill, "has made the hugest mistake ever committed by mortal man, or most anxious aspirant," a Democratic editor wrote. Another, writing in the *Ozaukee* (Wisconsin) *Times*, repudiated the paper's past support of Douglas when he ran for president in 1852. "Our cheek tingles with shame at the remembrance that we ever, in the remotest degree, assisted to add to the political prominence of so servile a doughface," the commentator wrote. Even some Missouri newspapers opposed the repeal of the compromise that made their territory a state. "Honorable men in Missouri feel that common honesty forbids their assailing, for selfish advantage, a compact of which they had had the benefit for a third of a century," the *New York Times* reported.

Proslavery forces did their best to push the legislation through Congress before the elections in November, when angry voters might replace those favoring the bill. Under Douglas's guidance, the bill took precedence over other legislation that had previously been scheduled for debate. The powerful senator steered the bill through the Senate and tried to cut off debate. He sold the bill through eloquent speeches. The West, he asserted, held the key to the nation's future and its prosperity.

Opponents made a last-ditch effort to turn the tide during the final debates before the vote. Representative Edmands of Massachusetts, in a lengthy speech delivered on May 20, 1854, urged his fellow congressmen to retain the Missouri Compromise and not give in to agitators who bore a

"Pandora's box" filled with "discord, dissension, and distrust." Edmands put southerners who pushed to repeal the Missouri Compromise in the same camp as northern abolitionists who lobbied for the immediate end of slavery. Both factions, he said, were political agitators whose actions threatened the unity of the nation. He warned that repealing the compromise would undercut all future efforts to negotiate peace between North and South on issues of bitter disagreement. If Congress passed the Douglas bill, he said, not only would the Missouri Compromise be struck down, "but the superstructure and foundation of every compromise [would] go with it, and no ground left whereon to construct another—nothing left to interpose between the southern institution and the sharp demands of the extremist of the North."

His words fell on deaf ears. On May 22, 1854, the House of Representatives approved the amended bill by a vote of 113 to 100. All but four of the Democrats from slave states—57— voted for the measure. They were joined by 43 Democrats from free states and 13 members of the Whig Party in slave states. Those opposing the bill included 43 Democrats from free states, 5 Whigs from slave states, 4 from the Free-Soil Party, and all 41 of the Whigs from free states.

Three days later the Senate followed suit, passing the measure on a vote of 35 to 13. The legislation established two territories, Nebraska and Kansas. The government of each territory included a governor appointed by the president, a judicial system, and a legislative assembly whose members were to be elected by citizens living in the region. The territories, like the states, would operate under the terms of the U.S. Constitution. Delegates to the U.S. House would represent the territories in Congress, but they would not get to vote. The most controversial section, the portion that allowed each territory to choose to enter the Union as a free state or a slave state, remained in the bill. According to the statement included in the legislation, the bill's "true intent" was not to "legislate slavery into any Territory or State, nor to exclude it therefrom, but to leave the people thereof perfectly free to form and regulate their domestic institutions in their own way, subject only to the Constitution of the United States." The new law also stipulated that the Fugitive Slave Act would be enforced in the region.

The passage of the bill annulled the Missouri Compromise's free state–slave state boundary, which had been in effect for the past thirty-four years. It also reignited the bitter conflict between North and South over the slavery issue that the 1850 compromise had attempted to settle. By the end of the decade those passions would erupt, propelling the nation into civil war.

"BLEEDING KANSAS"

Kansas had an estimated seven hundred soldiers and about the same number of white settlers living in it when it became an organized territory in 1854. Much of the land in both the Kansas and Nebraska territories belonged to various Indian tribes. The tribes lived on reservations set up there by treaties signed by the federal government. Once the effort began to organize the territory, the U.S. government—under pressure from powerful Missouri plantation owners—quietly negotiated new treaties that forced the tribes to cede their land and relocate farther west. That cleared the way for the neighboring Missourians and other whites to migrate west.

Hundreds of prominent Missourians poured into Kansas as soon as the Kansas-Nebraska bill passed. Even before the tribes had vacated the reservations, these new settlers

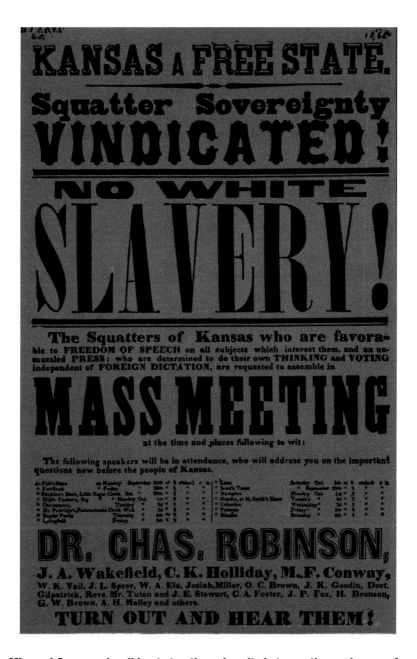

The Missouri Compromise did not stop the animosity between those who were for and those who were against slavery. This 1856 poster is an appeal to proslave farmers to rally against the abolition of slavery.

staked out claims to the land with the intention of boosting support for slavery in the new territory. For several years leading up to the passage of the Kansas-Nebraska Act, Missouri leaders had formed groups (Sons of the South, Social Bands, and others) to prepare for the migration west. Northerners, too, began sending groups to the new territories in an effort to build support for their antislavery stance.

The *Democratic Platform*, a Missouri newspaper, reported on June 8, 1854, that "a great many Missourians" had already arrived in Kansas in anticipation of the expected influx of settlers from the North. "Let every man that owns a negro go there [to Kansas] and settle, and our northern brethren will be compelled to hunt further north for a location," the writer exhorted. In another report later that month, the paper's editorial comments revealed the determination of the southerners to add Kansas as a slave state.

> We are in favor of making Kansas a "Slave State" if it should require half the citizens of Missouri, musket in hand, to emigrate there, and even sacrifice their lives in accomplishing so desirable an end.

Several southern newspapers of the time advised northerners not to settle in Kansas but to claim land in Nebraska instead. They warned their southern readers to stake out their claims as soon as possible before settlers from Massachusetts, whom they described as "cut-throats and murderers," arrived in the territory.

At the same time, northern newspapers enticed their readers with tantalizing descriptions of the fertile, beautiful land to be had for free in Kansas. Emigrant aid societies formed throughout the North to collect money and organize teams of would-be settlers whose sworn mission was to bring Kansas into the Union as a free state. In April 1854 the Massachusetts legislature granted a charter to the Massachusetts Emigrant Aid Company (later transformed into the New England Emigrant Aid Company) and allotted up to $5 million to aid in the settlement of Kansas by antislavery forces. The *New York Tribune* called the scheme "a plan for freedom." Other northern papers ran editorials boosting the Massachusetts proposal and encouraging readers to participate in the settlement of Kansas. New York and Connecticut soon followed suit, forming their own charter company in July. Private and public organizations created other emigration groups with the aim of flooding Kansas with antislavery settlers.

Much of the most desirable land had already been claimed by Missouri emigrants by the time the northern settlers arrived in Kansas, in midsummer 1854. A large contingent from the North settled in what today is Lawrence. Other antislavery settlers scattered throughout the region.

Missourians greeted this northern contingent with contempt. The *Democratic Platform* went so far as to suggest that Eli Thayer, president of the New England Emigrant Aid Society, deserved to be hanged. Another paper, the *Platte County Argus*, printed an advertisement offering a two hundred dollar reward to anyone who found and captured Thayer.

Organizers in Missouri formed secret "protection" groups to drive off emigrants from the northern aid societies and to extend slavery into western and northern regions. The violence between the two factions erupted into an internal war that became known as "Bleeding Kansas." But most of the new settlers devoted their time to building homes and preparing for the winter ahead.

During the first election for delegates to the Kansas assembly, armed members of the Missouri secret societies showed up at the polls to ensure that proslavery candidates won. They intimidated voters, cast ballots illegally, and otherwise tampered with the election results. The final tally gave the proslavery candidates, some of whom were Missouri residents, full control of the territory's legislature.

While the southern press applauded the fraud and cheered the election results, northern newspapers saw the Kansas situation as an omen of the coming "great battle between Freedom and Slavery." The territory's governor, Andrew Horatio Reeder, ignored death threats and set aside the results in several of the races and scheduled new elections for the disputed seats. As a result eight supporters of free-state status joined the legislature. Before conducting any other business, however, the legislature voted to unseat all the free-state candidates selected in the second election.

One of those ousted from his position, John A. Wakefield, spoke prophetically that Fourth of July 1855. "Gentlemen, this is a memorable day, and may become more so," he told the remaining legislators as he rose to leave the chambers. "Your acts will be the means of lighting the watch-fires of war in our land."

CHAPTER SEVEN

On the Way to War

A Supreme Court case involving the claims of a slave named Dred Scott delivered the final blow to the Missouri Compromise and savaged the antislavery cause. Scott began his ten-year court battle for freedom in 1847. Born as a slave in Virginia around 1800, Scott moved with his master to St. Louis, Missouri, in 1830. An army surgeon named John Emerson bought Scott and took him to Illinois, where slavery was banned. Nevertheless, Scott continued to work as a slave in Illinois for two and a half years. In 1836 Scott went with Emerson to Wisconsin Territory, another free area under the terms of the Missouri Compromise. There he married seventeen-year-old Harriet Robinson, also a slave. The couple had two daughters, Eliza and Lizzie. Four years later the Scotts moved to a St. Louis, Missouri, plantation owned by Mrs. Emerson's father. They spent the next several years working for a number of merchants who hired their labor from the Emersons. After John Emerson died in 1843, Scott tried to

The decision in the *Dred Scott* case delivered the final blow to any chance for a compromise on the issue of slavery. The ruling effectively took away all the rights of black people in the United States and further stirred up the conflict that led to civil war.

buy his family's freedom from Emerson's widow. When she refused to accept Scott's offer, Dred and Harriet Scott filed separate suits in St. Louis Circuit Court to win their freedom. Both suits were filed against Emerson's widow, Irene Emerson, who claimed ownership over the slave family, and her father, Alexander Sanford.

The Scotts, through their lawyer, argued that they should be freed from slavery because of their residence of several years in areas where slavery had been banned. Several other slaves had won their freedom in similar cases. In 1824 the Missouri Supreme Court had set the precedent, in the case of *Winny* v. *Whitesides*, that once a slave had been taken into free territory, he could no longer be enslaved. The state court's ruling in an 1837 case, *Rachel* v. *Walker*, decreed that the ban on slavery in northern territories applied to slaveholders serving in the military as well as those who were civilians.

The Missouri Supreme Court of the 1850s and later the U.S. Supreme Court of 1857, when the *Scott* case was finally decided, ultimately rejected such standards of justice, however. Instead, both courts bowed to the demands of those who favored the South and proslavery forces. The Missouri court used the two lawsuits (which became one case under the title *Dred Scott* v. *Irene Emerson*) to challenge the constitutionality of slavery bans in other sections of the country, historian Walter Ehrlich wrote. Its 2 to 1 ruling, issued on March 22, 1852, denied the Scotts' petition for freedom. Justice William Scott, author of the decision, claimed that while other territories and states might ban slavery, such laws had no effect in Missouri, where slavery was legal. Since the Scotts resided in Missouri, they came under that state's laws on slavery. The justice dismissed the validity of the court's previous rulings on the matter. "Times now are not as they were, when the former decisions on this subject were made," Justice Scott wrote. The ruling in effect denied the well-established understanding among states to honor each other's laws. It also challenged Congress's power to pass laws that affected the states.

Justice Hamilton Gamble, the one judge who dissented, took issue with Justice Scott's dismissal of time-honored rulings because of the changing times. "Times may have changed, public feeling may have changed, but principles have not and do not change, and in my judgment there can be no safe basis for judicial decisions, but in those principles which are immutable," Gamble wrote in his dissent.

After the decision, Irene Emerson's brother, John Sanford, took over control of the Scott family. Eventually the case, under the title *Dred Scott* v. *Sandford*, came before the U.S. Supreme Court (a clerk misspelled Sanford's name). The case unfolded on center stage amid the increasingly bitter dispute between the North and the South over slavery.

"THE ACT OF CONGRESS IS VOID"

The Supreme Court issued its ruling on the case on March 6, 1857. In a sweeping landmark decision written by Chief Justice Roger B. Taney, the Court not only rejected Scott's petition for freedom but also denied U.S. citizenship to all blacks, free or slave. The 7 to 2 ruling overturned the Missouri Compromise's ban on slavery in the northern territories, described slaves as property, and decreed that Congress had no power to restrict the spread of slavery to new states and territories. Two justices, John McLean of Ohio and Benjamin Robbins Curtis of Massachusetts, dissented from the opinion. A third, Justice Samuel Nelson of New York, issued a separate opinion that did not support the Court's ruling on the unconstitutionality of the Missouri Compromise. According to Taney's opinion, blacks were not included in the group of "people or citizens" guaranteed rights by the U.S. Constitution. Instead, they were "considered as a subordinate and inferior class of beings who had been subjugated by the dominant race, and, whether emancipated or not, yet remained subject to their authority, and had no rights or privileges but such as those who held the power and the Government might choose to grant them."

Since the Constitution recognized slaves as property, Taney wrote, Congress had no power to "exercise any more authority" over slaves than over "property of any other kind." Congress, he affirmed, infringed on states' rights when it passed a ban on slavery with the Missouri Compromise. "The act of Congress [Section 8 of the Missouri Compromise] which prohibited a citizen from holding and owning property of this kind [slaves] in the territory of the United States north of the line therein mentioned is not warranted by the Constitution, and is therefore void," Taney wrote. The decision left Dred and Harriet Scott and their two daughters enslaved. However, their owners freed the Scotts two months after the Court's ruling. The decision also left the antislavery ban of the Missouri Compromise no longer in effect.

Northern papers attacked the decision as racist and blatantly pro-South. "Sectionalism dead? It was the most intense, bitter, overshadowing sectionalism that forced this decree from the Supreme Court," wrote an editorial writer in the *New York Tribune*. The ruling outraged even northerners who did not favor abolition. They saw it as upsetting the balance of power, threatening white workers, and allowing slavery to spread throughout U.S. territory without limits. Dred

Slavery was among the major topics in the Lincoln-Douglas Senate debates of 1858. Douglas won the battle for the Senate, but he lost to Abraham Lincoln in the 1860 race for president.

Scott's case would be the last attempt to settle the slavery issue in the courts.

RESTORE THE COMPROMISE!

Far from settling the slavery issue, the U.S. Supreme Court's controversial decision in the *Dred Scott* case ignited the conflict. It became one of the central topics of the 1858 debates between Abraham Lincoln and Stephen Douglas. The two men conducted a series of debates during their campaign to represent Illinois in the Senate. Douglas won the race, but the debates propelled Lincoln into the public spotlight and eventually helped him win the 1860 presidential election.

During the debates Lincoln argued strongly against the repeal of the Missouri Compromise. Contrary to his opponent's claims, Lincoln maintained that the public had never called for a repeal of the 1820 law. He said that Congress should determine how to handle the slavery question in new territories as the situation arose. But, he contended, Nebraska's status as a free territory had been established thirty years prior, as part of the terms of the Missouri Compromise. To repeal the pact now, he charged, was to renege on the deal.

> It is as if two starving men had divided their only loaf; the one had hastily swallowed his half, and then grabbed the other half just as he was putting it to his mouth!

Central to the slavery dispute was the doctrine of states' rights. Supporters of the South contended that each state had the right to govern itself and make its own laws regarding slavery and other issues. Lincoln turned this argument around to bolster his cause.

[If] the negro is a man, is it not to that extent, a total destruction of self-government, to say that he too shall not govern himself? When the white man governs himself that is self-government; but when he governs himself, and also governs another man, that is more than self-government— that is despotism.

Lincoln also provided a strong defense of the 1787 Northwest Ordinance that had originally established the ban on slavery. He noted that Thomas Jefferson himself, "the most distinguished politician of our history," took the opportunity in writing the ordinance to stop the spread of slavery into the northwestern territory. The result, according to Lincoln, was five states with "five millions of free, enterprising people." He had nothing but scorn for critics who complained that the antislavery regulations in the ordinance "grossly violated" the "sacred right of self government" when a generation of Americans had prospered and continued to live worthwhile and productive lives under such rules.

We even find some men, who drew their first breath, and every other breath of their lives, under this very restriction, now live in dread of absolute suffocation, if they should be restricted in the "sacred right" of taking slaves to Nebraska. That perfect liberty they sigh for—the liberty of making slaves of other people—Jefferson never thought of; their own father never thought of; they never thought of themselves, a year ago. How fortunate for them, they did not sooner become sensible of their great misery!

For his part, Douglas tried to sway sympathies to his side of the argument by suggesting that Lincoln and his cronies were treating the white settlers of Nebraska unfairly. He accused Lincoln of saying, "The white people of Nebraska are good enough to govern themselves, but they are not good enough to govern a few miserable negroes!"

Lincoln countered with an assertion of his own, "that no man is good enough to govern another man, without that other's consent." The doctrine, he noted, formed the basis of the American republic, "that all men are created equal" and that the government derived its "just powers from the consent of the governed."

Lincoln noted that the entire nation had a stake in the development of the Nebraska Territory and that the decision to allow slavery in it should not rest solely with the residents who lived in the region at the moment. Once slaves were imported into the territory, wealthy plantation owners would take over the land. There would be no room for poor whites to settle and improve their lot, according to Lincoln. Moreover, the question of slavery—Lincoln called it "the great Behemoth of danger"—was too important to the welfare of the entire nation to leave in the hands of a few farmers whose vote reflected their own self-interest.

Congress had passed the Missouri Compromise because members believed it was the only way to preserve the Union. Lincoln contended that its repeal had done the opposite, threatening to reignite controversy in areas where the slavery question had been settled for three decades. "The Missouri Compromise was repealed," he said, "and here we are, in the midst of a new slavery agitation, such, I think, as we have never seen before."

A HOUSE DIVIDED

Evidence abounded that the question would not be settled peacefully. Already, even before Nebraska's government had established itself, abolitionists from the North began sending settlers to the region so they could oppose slavery there. Meanwhile, slaveholders in Missouri vowed to bring slaves into the territory. "Through all this," Lincoln exclaimed, "bowie-knives and six-shooters are seen plainly enough; but never a glimpse of the ballot-box."

The repeal of the Missouri Compromise signaled the end of the nation's willingness to compromise on controversial issues, according to Lincoln. "Who after this will ever trust in a national compromise?" he asked. By restoring the compromise, he said, Congress could avert a national crisis and "restore the national faith, the national confidence, the national feeling of brotherhood."

Slavery had always been considered an unfortunate necessity and tolerated only because the nation's economy depended on it, Lincoln said. The repeal of the Missouri Compromise and the acceptance of the Nebraska deal elevated slavery into a "sacred right." Such a doctrine—that slavery was a "sacred right of self-government"—stood at odds with the principle declared in the Declaration of Independence that "all men are created equal."

"These principles," Lincoln said, "can not stand together.... The spirit of seventy-six [1776] and the spirit of Nebraska, are utter antagonisms: and the former is being rapidly displaced by the latter."

Lincoln focused on the slavery issue in his acceptance speech, delivered on June 17, 1858, at the Republican State Convention in Springfield, Illinois, after the party nominated him as its candidate for U.S. Senate. Despite its stated goal of ending the national debate over slavery, the Kansas-Nebraska Act had stirred up the controversy, Lincoln said. He correctly predicted that it would take a crisis to settle the matter, although he said that he did not expect the Union to dissolve over it. "A house divided against itself cannot stand," he declared. "I believe this government cannot endure permanently half slave and half free."

His opponent in the senatorial race, Stephen A. Douglas, would refer to Lincoln's words frequently in the upcoming debates. Douglas tried to paint Lincoln as an abolitionist who clamored for war against the slaveholding southern states. Lincoln, for his part, denied the charge, saying that he opposed slavery but found no constitutional ground to interfere with the institution in states where it had existed long before the nation's founding. Back then, Lincoln noted, Americans held the view that slavery was wrong and should be ended someday, but individual states needed it to survive economically. Those who opposed slavery could live with its existence as long as they believed the ultimate goal of the nation was to eliminate it, according to Lincoln. The trouble began, he asserted, when slaveholders abandoned that philosophy and began to portray slavery as being a good thing.

WAR AND AN END TO SLAVERY

Abraham Lincoln won the presidential election of 1860 because southern voters split their support among national Democratic Party candidate Stephen A. Douglas, the southern Democrat candidate John C. Breckinridge, and John Bell, the Constitutional Union Party candidate. Lincoln beat out his opponents with slightly less than 40 percent of the popular vote and 180 of 303 Electoral College votes—none from the South.

The firing of the Confederate guns on Fort Sumter on April 12, 1861, marked the beginning of the nation's civil war.

The campaign and Lincoln's election further united southern states and strained relations between North and South to the breaking point. In December 1860, a month after Lincoln's election to the presidency, South Carolina seceded from the Union. Six other states seceded in the next two months. By mid–1861 twelve southern states had left the Union and formed the Confederate States of America. With the firing of Confederate guns on Fort Sumter in Charleston, South Carolina, on April 12, 1861, the Civil War began.

In 1863 President Lincoln signed the Emancipation Proclamation, which freed the slaves in the Confederate states. The

Union victory two years later and the Thirteenth Amendment, ratified in 1865, ended slavery in America. The first section of the Fourteenth Amendment finally overturned the *Dred Scott* opinion. With the passage of the amendment, ratified in 1868, "all persons born or naturalized in the United States," including former slaves, became citizens of the United States and of the state where they lived.

From Bill to Law

For a proposal to become a federal law, it must go through many steps:

In Congress:

1. A bill is proposed by a citizen, a legislator, the president, or another interested party. Most bills originate in the House and then are considered in the Senate.

2. A representative submits the bill to the House (the first reading). A senator submits it to the Senate. The person (or people) who introduces the bill is its main sponsor. Other lawmakers can become sponsors to show support for the bill. Each bill is read three times before the House or the Senate.

3. The bill is assigned a number and referred to the committee(s) and subcommittee(s) dealing with the topic. Each committee adopts its own rules, following guidelines of the House and the Senate. The committee chair controls scheduling for the bill.

4. The committees hold hearings if the bill is controversial or complex. Experts and members of the public may testify. Congress may compel witnesses to testify if they do not do so voluntarily.

5. The committee reviews the bill, discusses it, adds amendments, and makes other changes it deems necessary during markup sessions.

6. The committee votes on whether to support the bill, oppose it, or take no action on it and issues a report on its findings and recommendations.

7. A bill receiving a favorable committee report goes to the Rules Committee to be scheduled for consideration by the full House or Senate.

8. If the committee delays a bill or if the Rules Committee fails to schedule it, House members can sign a discharge motion and call for a vote on the matter. If a majority votes to release the bill from committee, it is scheduled on the calendar as any other bill would be. Senators may vote to discharge the bill from a committee as well. More commonly, though, a senator will add the bill as an amendment to an unrelated bill in order to get it past the committee blocking it. Or a senator can request that a bill be put directly on the Senate calendar, where it will be scheduled for debate. House and Senate members can also vote to suspend the rules and vote directly on a bill. Bills passed in this way must receive support from two thirds of those voting.

9. Members of both houses debate the bill. In the House, a chairperson moderates the discussion and each speaker's time is limited. Senators can speak on the issue for as long as they wish. Senators who want to block the bill may debate for hours in a tactic known as a filibuster. A three-fifths vote of the Senate is required to stop the filibuster (cloture), and talk on the bill is then limited to one hour per senator.

10. Following the debate, the bill is read section by section (the second reading). Members may propose amendments, which are voted on before the final bill comes up for a vote.

11. The full House and Senate then debate the entire bill and those amendments approved previously. Debate continues until a majority of members vote to "move the previous question" or approve a special resolution forcing a vote.

12. A full quorum—at least 218 members in the House, 51 in the Senate—must be present for a vote to be held. A member may request a formal count of members to ensure a quorum is on hand. Absent members are sought when there is no quorum.

13. Before final passage, opponents are given a last chance to propose amendments that alter the bill; the members vote on them.

14. A bill needs approval from a majority of those voting to pass. Members who do not want to take a stand on the issue may choose to abstain (not vote at all) or merely vote present.

15. If the House passes the bill, it goes on to the Senate. By that time, bills often have more than one hundred amendments attached to them. Occasionally, a Senate bill will go to the House.

16. If the bill passes in the same form in both the House and the Senate, it is sent to the clerk to be recorded.

17. If the Senate and the House version differ, the Senate sends the bill to the House with the request that members approve the changes.

18. If the two houses disagree on the changes, the bill may go to conference, where members appointed by the House and the Senate work out a compromise if possible.

19. The House and the Senate vote on the revised bill agreed to in conference. Further amendments may be added and the process repeated if the Senate and the House version of the bill differ.

20. The bill goes to the president for a signature.

To the President:

1. If the president signs the bill, it becomes law.

2. If the president vetoes the bill, it goes back to Congress, which can override his veto with a two-thirds vote in both houses.

3. If the president takes no action, the bill automatically becomes law after ten days if Congress is still in session.

4. If Congress adjourns and the president has taken no action on the bill within ten days, the bill does not become law. This is known as a pocket veto.

The time from introduction of the bill to the signing can range from several months to the entire two-year session. If a bill does not win approval during the session, it can be reintroduced in the next Congress, where it will have to go through the entire process again.

Notes

Introduction

p. 8, "mere party trick," Joshua Michael Zeitz, "The Missouri Compromise Reconsidered: Antislavery Rhetoric and the Emergence of the Free Labor Synthesis," *Journal of the Early Republic*, 20 (Fall 2000), Society for Historians of the Early American Republic, 447–485. Citing Thomas Jefferson letter to Charles Pinckney, September 30, 1820.

p. 9, "The repeal . . . ," Robert Pierce Forbes, *The Missouri Compromise and Its Aftermath*, Chapel Hill, NC: University of North Carolina Press, 2007, 275.

p. 10, "The Missouri Compromise," Ourdocuments.gov, www.ourdocuments.gov/ doc.php?flash=true&doc=22

Chapter One

p. 15, "Under the terms . . . 'liberty,'" "Northwest Ordinance of 1787," Ourdocuments. gov, www.ourdocuments.gov/doc.php?doc=8

p. 19, "an event so portentous . . . ," Henry Adams, *History of the United States of America During the Administrations of Thomas Jefferson*, New York: The Library of America, 1986, 334–335.

p. 21, "under tollarable good . . . ," University of Nebraska Press/University of Nebraska–Lincoln Libraries–Electronic Text Center (March 2005). *The Journals of the Lewis and Clark Expedition*, week of Sept. 21–Sept. 23, 1806. http://lewis andclarkjournals.unl.edu/read/?_xmlsrc=1806-09-23.xml&_xslsrc=LCstyles.xsl

p. 21, "the fulfillment of our manifest destiny . . . ," R. A. Guisepi, ed., "Manifest Destiny," International World History Project, 2004. http://history-world.org/ westward_movement.htm

p. 22, "2 million pounds of cotton . . . ," J. Lawrence Broz, "The United States in the World Economy, 1800–1900," lecture, University of California at San Diego. http://dss.ucsd.edu/~jlbroz/Courses/POLI142B/lecture/1800-1900.pdf

p. 22, "Cotton literally exploded . . . ," Public Broadcasting Service, "Douglas Egerton on the 'positive good' theory of slavery," Africans in America series. PBS. www.pbs.org/wgbh/aia/part3/3i3113.html

p. 23, "Georgia's charter . . . ," Library of Congress, "The African–American Mosaic." www.loc.gov/exhibits/african/afam005.html

p. 25, "almost 700,000 slaves . . . ," Douglas Harper, "Slavery in the North," 2003. www.slavenorth.com/author.htm

p. 26, "U.S. Political Parties, 1780–1860," Edgate.com. "Copernicus Election Watch: The Parties." *USA Today*, 2000. www.edgate.com/elections/inactive/the_parties

p. 27, "After the War of 1812 . . . ," "House History," Office of the Clerk, U.S. House of Representatives. http://clerk.house.gov/art_history/house_history/index.html

Chapter Two

p. 31, "more than 76,000 people . . . ," U.S. Census Bureau," "Resident Population and Apportionment of the U.S. House of Representatives: Louisiana." www.census.gov/dmd/www/resapport/states/louisiana.pdf

pp. 32–33, "one of the finest . . . ," St. Louis Walk of Fame. "St. Louis Walk of Fame: Pierre Laclède." http://stlouiswalkoffame.org/inductees/pierre-laclede.html

p. 33, "one hundred steamboats . . . ," "St. Louis History," St. Louis Convention & Visitors Commission, June 2, 2008. www.explorestlouis.com/media/pressKit/stLouisHistory.asp

p. 33, "In the decade . . . ," U.S. Census Bureau, "Resident Population and Apportionment of the U.S. House of Representatives: Louisiana." www.census.gov/dmd/www/resapport/states/louisiana.pdf

p. 34, "like a firebell . . . ," Thomas Jefferson, *Thomas Jefferson Papers*, Letter to John Holmes, April 22, 1820, American Memory Historical Collections, Library of Congress. www.loc.gov/rr/program/bib/ourdocs/Missouri.html

p. 35, "a wolf by the ears . . . ," David Grubin, dir., "The Time of the Lincolns," *American Experience*, WGBH/Public Broadcasting Service. www.pbs.org/wgbh/amex/lincolns/politics/es_shift.html

p. 36, "threats of breaking up . . . ," Abraham Lincoln, Speech on the Repeal of the Missouri Compromise, Peoria, Illinois, October 16, 1854. Recorded at the Ashbrook Center for Public Affairs at Ashland University. www.ashbrook.org/library/19/lincoln/peoria.html

p. 37, "Representative John W. Taylor . . . 'be applied to it,'" *Annals of Congress*, 15th Cong., House, 2nd sess., 1170 (1819).

p. 39, "It is much to be wished . . . ," Jake Sudderth, "The Papers of John Jay," Columbia University Libraries, 2002. www.columbia.edu/cu/lweb/digital/jay/JaySlavery.html

p. 39, "lamentable evil" and "an abhorrence of slavery," Steve Mount, "Constitutional Topic: Slavery," USConstitution.net, April 25, 2007. www.usconstitution.net/consttop_slav.html

p. 40, "Abraham Lincoln suggested . . . United States," Lincoln, Speech on the Repeal of the Missouri Compromise.

p. 41, (Barbour) "'This term' . . . original states did," *Annals of Congress*, 15th Cong., House, 2nd sess., 1185–1191 (1819).

pp. 41–42, (Fuller) "We hold . . . purely republican . . . born free . . . It clearly . . . republican," *Annals of Congress*, 15th Cong., House, 2nd sess., 1170 (1819).

p. 42, (Taylor) "Gentlemen have now . . . ," *Annals of Congress*, 15th Cong., House, 2nd sess., 1174 (1819).

p. 43, "That was a new idea . . . ," Public Broadcasting Service, "Douglas Egerton on the 'positive good' theory of slavery."

p. 43, (Walker) "They hear the term slave . . . ," *Annals of Congress*, 16th Cong., Senate, 1st sess., 173 (1820).

p. 43, (Smith) "there is no class . . .," *Annals of Congress*, 16th Cong., Senate, 1st sess., 268 (1820).

pp. 43, 46, "Senator Benjamin Ruggles . . . be suggested," *Annals of Congress*, 16th Cong., Senate, 1st sess., 279 (1820).

pp. 44–45, "Life as a Slave," Nicholas Boston, "The Slave Experience: Living Conditions," *Slavery and the Making of America*, Public Broadcasting Service, Educational Broadcasting Corp., 2004. www.pbs.org/wnet/slavery/experience/living/history2.html

p. 46, "Speaker of the House Clay . . . other necessities," *Annals of Congress*, 15th Cong., 2nd sess., 1175 (1819).

p. 46, "An unimpressed Taylor . . .," *Annals of Congress*, 15th Cong., House, 2nd sess., 1175–1282 (1819).

p. 46, (Livermore) "slaves existed . . . 'in chains!'", *Annals of Congress*, 15th Cong., 2nd sess., 1175 (1819).

p. 46, "with considerable spirit," *Annals of Congress*, 15th Cong., House, 2nd sess., 1175 (1819).

p. 47, (Cobb) "the Union will be dissolved . . . , " *Annals of Congress*, 15th Cong., House, 2nd sess., 1175 (1819).

p. 47, (Tallmadge) "If a dissolution . . . , " *Annals of Congress*, 15th Cong., House, 2nd sess., 1175 (1819).

p. 47, "We must go on . . . ," Forbes, *The Missouri Compromise and Its Aftermath*, 46.

p. 47, "gave rise to . . . ," *Annals of Congress*, 15th Cong., Senate, 2nd sess., 273 (1819).

pp. 48–49, "The following Monday . . . threats of civil war," *Annals of Congress*, 15th Cong., Senate, 2nd sess., 280 (1819).

Chapter Three

p. 52, "Maine, with a population . . . ," Eva Murphy, Reference Librarian, State Library of Massachusetts, Boston.

pp. 52–53, "Shall Maine be a free . . . ," Independence broadside, July 21, 1819, transcribed from the original by Earlene Ahlquist Chadbourne, Dyer Library Saco Museum archives.

pp. 54, 56, "Senator Jonathan Roberts . . . not been settled," *Annals of Congress*, 16th Cong., Senate, 1st sess., 119–153 (1820).

p. 56, "The fact that 'the people of Maine' ... 'admit neither,'" *Annals of Congress*, 16th Cong., Senate, 1st sess., 94–118 (1820).

p. 57, (Barbour) "The same spirit ... ," *Annals of Congress*, 16th Cong., Senate, 1st sess., 1820, 94.

p. 58, (Elliott) "One-half of the States ... 'the Union,'" 16th Cong., Senate, 1st sess., 130 (1820).

p. 58, (Morril) "stamina, nerve, ... we fall," *Annals of Congress*, 16th Cong., Senate, 1st sess., 137 (1820).

pp. 58–59, "While the debate ... and slave states," Robert Pierce Forbes, *The Missouri Compromise and Its Aftermath*, 64–65.

p. 59, "full force and effect ... ," *Annals of Congress*, 16th Cong., Senate, 1st sess., 158 (1820).

p. 60, (Walker) "a storm portending ... ," *Annals of Congress*, 16th Cong., Senate, 1st sess., 175 (1820).

p. 60, (Mellen) "I have better ... ," *Annals of Congress*, 16th Cong., Senate, 1st sess., 177 (1820).

p. 62, "Senator Ninian Edwards ... tolerated slavery," *Annals of Congress*, 16th Cong., Senate, 1st sess., 188–189 (1820).

p. 63, (Lowrie) "'In the nine' ... of the United States," *Annals of Congress*, 16th Cong., Senate, 1st sess., 208–209 (1820).

pp. 63–64, (Macon) "disturb and distract ... of the United States," *Annals of Congress*, 16th Cong., Senate, 1st sess., 220–232 (1820).

pp. 64, 66, (Otis) "With a touch ... 'and independence,'" *Annals of Congress*, 16th Cong., Senate, 1st sess., 250–254 (1820).

p. 66, (Van Dyke) "'The proposed restriction' ... other state powers," *Annals of Congress*, 16th Cong., Senate, 1st sess., 300–310 (1820).

p. 66, "blot on the national character," *Annals of Congress*, 16th Cong., Senate, 1st sess., 387 (1820).

Chapter Four

p. 67, (Burrill) "in great part ... ," *Annals of Congress*, 16th Cong., Senate, 1st sess., 380–381 (1820).

p. 68, (King) "absolutely void ... law of God," *Annals of Congress*, 16th Cong., Senate, 1st sess., 380–381 (1820).

pp. 68, 71, (Smith) "the religion ... known to man," *Annals of Congress*, 16th Cong., Senate, 1st sess., 382 (1820).

p. 70, "William Pinkney of Maryland ... 'in political power.'" *Annals of Congress*, 16th Cong., Senate, 1st sess., 413 (1820).

p. 70, "their privileges ... their proper sphere," cited in Forbes, *The Missouri Compromise and Its Aftermath*, 113.

p. 71, (Pinkney) "astonishment," *Annals of Congress*, 16th Cong., Senate, 1st sess., 389–90 (1820).

p. 71, "The attempt to impose . . . by both sides," *Annals of Congress*, 16th Cong., 1st sess., Senate 389–394 (1820).

p. 72, "In his remarks Meigs . . . 'comfort and happiness,'" *Annals of Congress*, 16th Cong., House, 1st sess., 113–114 (1820).

p. 72, "the resolution sent . . . ," Forbes, *The Missouri Compromise and Its Aftermath*, 68.

p. 73, "Initially the representatives . . . on the House," 16th Cong., House, 1st sess., House, 1406–1426 (1820).

p. 73, (Scott) "present prosperity . . . ," 16th Cong., House, 1st sess., 1491–1541 (1820).

pp. 74–75, "Representative Thomas Forrest . . . over the issue," 16th Cong., House, 1st sess., 1559–1564 (1820).

p. 75, (Randolph) "unconstitutional and unjust. . . ," 16th Cong., House, 1st sess., 1569–1571 (1820).

p. 76, (Clay) "for one . . . subject," 16th Cong., House, 1st sess., 1576 (1820).

p. 76, "Benjamin Adams . . . 'tranquility to the country.'" 16th Cong., House, 1st sess., 1578 (1820).

pp. 76–77, "They promoted . . . pass the bill," Forbes, *The Missouri Compromise and Its Aftermath*, 69–71, 77, 92–95.

p. 77, "Representative Charles Kinsey . . . cheaper imports," Forbes, *The Missouri Compromise and Its Aftermath*, 97.

pp. 77–78, "Explaining his change . . . 'rests upon us,'" 16th Cong., House, 1st sess., 1578–1582 (1820).

p. 78, "Representative James Stevens . . . 'ardor of patriotism,'" 16th Cong., House, 1st sess., 1586 (1820).

p. 79, (Randolph) "doughfaces . . . ," Forbes, *The Missouri Compromise and Its Aftermath*, 98.

pp. 79–80, "The first seven . . . into free territory," Missouri Compromise.

p. 80, "I have never . . . the present one," James Monroe letter to Thomas Jefferson, February 19, 1820, *The Writings of James Monroe: Including a Collection of His Public and Private Papers and Correspondence Now for the First Time Printed*, New York: G. P. Putnam's Sons, 1902, 116.

p. 80, "When the president . . . constitutional," "The Missouri Compromise," Son necessities of the South website. www.sonofthesouth.net/slavery/missouri-compromise.htm

Chapter Five

pp. 82–83, "A young man . . . white laborers," Richard Hooker, "Slave Rebellions," The African Diaspora, Washington State University, 1996. www.wsu.edu/~dee/DIASPORA/REBEL.HTM

p. 83, "He aimed . . . out of the state," "Gabriel's Conspiracy, 1799–1800," *Africans in America* series, Public Broadcasting Service, WGBH Education Foundation,

1998, 1999. www.pbs.org/wgbh/aia/part3/3p1576.html

p. 83, (Burrill) "a confederacy. . . ," 16th Cong., Senate, 2nd sess., 47 (1820).

p. 85, "Senator William Smith . . . Missouri's constitution," 16th Cong., Senate, 2nd sess., 51–77 (1820).

p. 86, "Missouri would be required . . . 'of this Union,'" 16th Cong., House, 2nd sess., 1080 (1821).

p. 86, "Several Missouri . . . their constitution," Forbes, *The Missouri Compromise and Its Aftermath*, 108–109.

p. 86, "Representative Gideon Tomlinson . . . 'sworn to support,'" 16th Cong., House, 2nd sess., 1095 (1821).

p. 87, "The unsettled issue . . . Missouri's statehood," Forbes, *The Missouri Compromise and Its Aftermath*, 115–116.

pp. 87–88, "Representative Charles Pinckney . . . 'people of that State?'" Forbes, *The Missouri Compromise and Its Aftermath*, 114–115.

p. 88, "He alternately . . . resolution before it," 16th Cong., House, 2nd sess., 1145 (1821).

p. 88, "When the matter . . . of the bargain," 16th Cong., House, 2nd sess., 1197–1201 (1821).

pp. 88–89, "They believed . . . antislavery candidates," Forbes, *The Missouri Compromise and Its Aftermath*, 117.

p. 90, "shall never be . . . the United States," Isidor Loeb, *Constitutions and Constitutional Conventions in Missouri*, Columbia, Missouri: State Historical Society of Missouri, 1920, 8.

p. 90, "hushed . . . deeper and deeper," Thomas Jefferson, *Thomas Jefferson Papers*. Letter to John Holmes, April 22, 1820, American Memory Historical Collections, Library of Congress. www.loc.gov/rr/program/bib/ourdocs/Missouri.html

Chapter Six

p. 91, "We scarcely ever . . . a bitterer cup," John C. Waugh, *On the Brink of Civil War: The Compromise of 1850 and How It Changed the Course of American History*, Lanham, MD: Rowman & Littlefield, 2003, 13.

p. 91, "a great triumph," Forbes, *The Missouri Compromise and Its Aftermath*, 98.

p. 92, "We have gained . . . it has cost us," Forbes, *The Missouri Compromise and Its Aftermath*, 99.

p. 92, "Rufus King confided . . . 'of [their] citizens,'" Rufus King and Charles Rufus King, *The Life and Correspondence of Rufus King*, New York: G.P. Putnam's Sons, 1899, 289.

p. 92, "John Quincy Adams . . . 'is laid asleep,'" Henry Adams and Charles Francis, ed., *Memoirs of John Quincy Adams, Comprising Portions of his Diary from 1795 to 1848*, vol. 5, Philadelphia: J.B. Lippincott & Co., 1875, 4–12.

p. 93, "Senator John F. Parrot . . . 'promoted it,'" "Nebraska" editorial, *New York Tribune* (January 23, 1854). Cited by Secession Era Editorials Project. http://history.

furman.edu/editorials/showsearched.py?kw=senator&ecode=nytrkn540123a

p. 94, "that great patriotic measure . . . enough to disturb,"Stephen A. Douglas, Speech on the Repeal of the Missouri Compromise.

p. 96, "it was necessary . . . of [the] country," Thomas Ritchie, "Mr. Clay and the Compromise," *New York Times* (September 18, 1852), 3.

p. 97, "The commissioner . . . 'into Indian families,'" Appendix to the *Congressional Globe*, 33rd Congress, Senate, 1st sess., 753 (1854).

p. 97, "Along the eastern . . . 87,000 slaves," William G. Cutler, *History of the State of Kansas*, Chicago, IL.: A. T. Andreas, 1883. www.kancoll.org/books/cutler/terrhist/terrhist-p1.html#POPULATION

p. 98, "I know no South . . . my own State," Henry Clay, *The Works of Henry Clay*, New York: Barnes & Burr, 1863, 207.

p. 98, "Historians have . . . Union together," Thomas Rush, "Henry Clay (1777–1852)," *From Revolution to Reconstruction*, Department of Alfa-Information, University of Groningen (The Netherlands). www.let.rug.nl/usa/B/hclay/hclay.htm

p. 99, "It has been my invariable . . . to my heart," Thomas Rush, "Henry Clay (1777–1852)," *From Revolution to Reconstruction*, Department of Alfa-Information, University of Groningen (The Netherlands). www.let.rug.nl/usa/B/hclay/hclay.htm

p. 100, "An article published . . . by 5 percent," "A Tour in the Southwest: The Nebraska Question in Texas," *New York Times* (May 13, 1854), 2.

p. 101, "Representative Alfred H. Colquitt . . . 'sanctuary of the States,'" Appendix to the *Congressional Globe*, 33rd Congress, House, 1st sess., 751 (1854).

p. 101, "slave states occupied . . . in free states," 1850 census, cited by Edmands, Appendix to the *Congressional Globe*, 33rd Congress, House, 1st sess., 754 (1854).

pp. 101–102, "The more this Nebraska . . . third of a century," "The Nebraska Question in the Northwestern States," *New York Times* (March 8, 1854), 2.

p. 103, "Pandora's box . . . extremist of the North," Appendix to the *Congressional Globe*, 33rd Congress, House, 1st sess., 755 (1854).

p. 104, "the bill's 'true intent'. . . the United States," "An Act to Organize the Territories of Nebraska and Kansas," *United States Statutes at Large: Treaties of the United States of America*, v. 10, Boston: Little Brown, 1855, 277. www.vlib.us/amdocs/texts/kanneb.html

pp. 104, 106, "Kansas had an estimated . . . their antislavery stance," William G. Cutler, "Territorial History," *History of the State of Kansas*. www.kancoll.org/books/cutler/terrhist/terrhist-p2.html

p. 106, "The *Democratic Platform* . . . 'desirable an end,'" *Democratic Platform*, Liberty, Missouri (June 27, 1854), cited in Cutler, "Territorial History."

p. 106, "cut-throats and murderers," Cutler, "Territorial History."

p. 108, "While the southern . . . second election," *New York Tribune*, April 19, 1855, cited in Cutler, "Territorial History."

p. 108, "Gentlemen, this is . . . in our land," Cutler, "Territorial History."

Chapter Seven

pp. 109, 111, "A Supreme Court case . . . who were civilians," "Missouri's Dred Scott Case, 1846–1857," Missouri Digital Heritage. www.sos.mo.gov/archives/resources/africanamerican/scott/scott.asp

p. 111, "The Missouri court . . . of the country," Walter Ehrlich, *They Have No Rights: Dred Scott's Struggle for Freedom*, Westport, CT: Greenwood Press, 1979, 58, cited in "Missouri's Dred Scott Case, 1846–1857."

p. 112, "Times now are . . . subject were made," "Missouri's Dred Scott Case, 1846–1857."

p. 112, "Times may have changed . . . which are immutable," Justice Hamilton Gamble, dissent, *Scott* v. *Emerson*, cited in "Missouri's Dred Scott Case, 1846–1857."

p. 113, "According to Taney's . . . 'is therefore void,'" *Scott* v. *Sandford*, 60 U.S. 393 (1856). http://supreme.justia.com/us/60/393/case.html

p. 113, "The decision left . . . the Court's ruling," "Missouri's Dred Scott Case, 1846–1857."

p. 113, "Sectionalism dead? . . . the Supreme Court," *New York Tribune*, March 21, 1857, cited in "Missouri's Dred Scott Case, 1846–1857."

p. 113, "The ruling outraged . . . without limits," "Missouri's Dred Scott Case, 1846–1857."

pp. 115–118, "It is as if two starving . . . displaced by the latter," Abraham Lincoln, Speech on the Repeal of the Missouri Compromise.

p. 119, "A house divided . . . and half free," Abraham Lincoln, Republican State Convention speech, June 16, 1858.

p. 121, "all persons . . . United States," U.S. Constitution, Amendment XIV, Sect. 1.

From Bill to Law

pp. 122–125, "From Bill to Law," Bernard Asbell, *The Senate Nobody Knows*, Baltimore: Johns Hopkins University Press, 1978; Charles W. Johnson, "How Our Laws Are Made," Washington, D.C.: U.S. Government Printing Office, 1998; and "Measures of Congressional Workload," CongressLink, The Dirksen Congressional Center, www.congresslink.org/print_basics_histmats_workloadstats.htm

All websites accessible as of October 3, 2009.

Further Information

Books

Altman, Linda Jacobs. *The Politics of Slavery: Fiery National Debates Fueled by the Slave Economy*. Berkeley Heights, NJ: Enslow Publishers, 2004.

Ball, Lea. *The Federalist-Anti-Federalist Debate over States' Rights: A Primary Source Investigation*. New York: Rosen Publishing Group, 2004.

Banks, Joan. *The U.S. Constitution*. Broomall, PA: Chelsea House Publications, 2001.

Barber, Benjamin R. *A Passion for Democracy*. Princeton, NJ: Princeton University Press, 2000.

Barber, Nathan. *Get Wise! Mastering U.S. History*. Lawrenceville, NJ: Peterson's Guides, 2004.

Burgan, Michael. *Henry Clay: The Great Compromiser*. North Mankato, MN: Child's World, 2004.

Horton, James Oliver, and Lois E. Horton. *Slavery and the Making of America*. New York: Oxford University Press, 2006.

Jordan, Anne Devereaux, with Virginia Schomp. *Slavery and Resistance*. New York: Benchmark Books, 2006.

McArthur, Debra. *The Kansas-Nebraska Act and Bleeding Kansas*. Berkeley Heights, NJ: Enslow Publishers, 2003.

Reef, Catherine. *This Our Dark Country: The American Settlers of Liberia*. Boston: Clarion Books, 2002.

Torr, James D., ed. *Slavery*. San Diego: Greenhaven Press, 2003.

Audio/Video

Bell, Edward, and Thomas Lennon. *Unchained Memories: Readings from the Slave Narratives*. HBO Home Video, 2003.

Causes of the Civil War, Schlessinger Media, 2003.

Greene, David, Gilbert Moses, John Erman, and Marvin J. Chomsky, dir. *Roots*, 1977. Based on the book by Alex Haley. Warner Home Video, 2007.

WEBSITES

America.gov
http://uspolitics.america.gov/uspolitics/government/index.html

American Memory
http://memory.loc.gov/ammem/index.html

From Revolution to Reconstruction
www.let.rug.nl/usa

Landmark Cases of the U.S. Supreme Court
www.landmarkcases.org

The Lincoln-Douglas Debates of 1858
www.nps.gov/liho/historyculture/debates.htm

National Archives
www.archives.gov

Our Documents Initiative
www.ourdocuments.gov/index.php?flash=true&

Primary Documents in American History
www.loc.gov/rr/program/bib/ourdocs/Missouri.html

Social Studies for Kids
www.socialstudiesforkids.com/articles/ushistory/missouricompromise1.htm

Son of the South
www.sonofthesouth.net/slavery/missouri-compromise.htm

U.S. House of Representatives
www.house.gov

U.S. Senate
www.senate.gov

All websites accessible as of October 3, 2009.

Bibliography

ARTICLES

Anonymous. Essay, *Daily National Intelligencer*, November 20, 1819.

Boston, Nicholas. "The Slave Experience: Living Conditions," *Slavery and the Making of America*, Public Broadcasting Service, Educational Broadcasting Corp., 2004. www.pbs.org/wnet/slavery/experience/living/history2.html

Broz, J. Lawrence. "The United States in the World Economy, 1800–1900," lecture, University of California at San Diego. http://dss.ucsd.edu/~jlbroz/Courses/ POLI142B/lecture/1800-1900.pdf

Dirksen Congressional Center. "Senate Workload/House Workload, 1947–2000." www.congresslink.org/print_basics_histmats_workloadstats.htm

"The Era of Good Feelings: The Growth of Political Factionalism and Sectionalism," Digital History, University of Houston, August 12, 2008. www.digital history. uh.edu/database/article_display.cfm?HHID=574

"House History." Office of the Clerk, U.S. House of Representatives. http://clerk. house.gov/art_history/house_history/index.html

Independence Broadside, July 21, 1819, transcribed from the original by Earlene Ahlquist Chadbourne, Dyer Library/Saco Museum archives.

Jefferson, Thomas. Letter to Charles Pinckney, September 30, 1820.

——. Thomas Jefferson Papers. Letter to John Holmes, April 22, 1820. American Memory Historical Collections, Library of Congress. www.loc.gov/rr/program /bib/ourdocs/Missouri.html

Library of Congress, "The African–American Mosaic." www.loc.gov/exhibits /african/afam005.html

"The Missouri Crisis 1819–1821, March 6, 1997," Skidmore College. www.skidmore. edu/academics/history/courses/OLD_TAD/hi323/Missouri.htm

"Missouri's Dred Scott Case, 1846–1857." Missouri Digital Heritage. www.sos. mo.gov/archives/resources/africanamerican/scott/scott.asp

Mount, Steve. "Constitutional Topic: Slavery," USConstitution.net, April 25, 2007. www.usconstitution.net/consttop_slav.html

"Nebraska," editorial. *New York Tribune*, January 23, 1854. Cited by Secession Era Editorials Project. http://history.furman.edu/editorials/showsearched.py?kw=senator&ecode=nytrkn540123a

"The Nebraska Question in the Northwestern States." *New York Times*, March 8, 1854, 2.

Public Broadcasting Service. "Douglas Egerton on the 'positive good' theory of slavery," *Africans in America* series. PBS. www.pbs.org/wgbh/aia/part3/3i3113.html

Ritchie, Thomas. "Mr. Clay and the Compromise." *New York Times*, September 18, 1852, 3.

Rush, Thomas. "Henry Clay (1777–1852), From Revolution to Reconstruction," Department of Alfa-Information, University of Groningen (The Netherlands). www.let.rug.nl/usa/B/hclay/hclay.htm

St. Louis Walk of Fame. "St. Louis Walk of Fame: Pierre Laclède." http://stlouiswalkoffame.org/inductees/pierre-laclede.html

Sudderth, Jake. "The Papers of John Jay," Columbia University Libraries, 2002. www.columbia.edu/cu/lweb/digital/jay/JaySlavery.html

"A Tour in the Southwest: The Nebraska Question in Texas." *New York Times*, May 13, 1854, 2.

U.S. Census Bureau, "Resident Population and Apportionment of the U.S. House of Representatives: Louisiana." www.census.gov/dmd/www/resapport/states/louisiana.pdf

Zeitz, Joshua Michael. "The Missouri Compromise Reconsidered: Antislavery Rhetoric and the Emergence of the Free Labor Synthesis," *Journal of the Early Republic*, 20 (Fall 2000), Society for Historians of the Early American Republic.

Audio/Video

Grubin, David, director. "The Time of the Lincolns," *American Experience*, WGBH/Public Broadcasting Service. www.pbs.org/wgbh/amex/lincolns/politics/es_shift.html

Lincoln, Abraham. "Speech on the Repeal of the Missouri Compromise, Peoria, Illinois, October 16, 1854." Recorded at the Ashbrook Center for Public Affairs at Ashland University. www.ashbrook.org/library/19/lincoln/peoria.html

Books/Booklets

Adams, Henry. *History of the United States of America During the Administrations of Thomas Jefferson*, New York: The Library of America, 1986.

Adams, Henry, and Charles Francis, ed. *Memoirs of John Quincy Adams, Comprising Portions of his Diary from 1795 to 1848*, vol. 5, Philadelphia: J. B. Lippincott & Co., 1875.

Clay, Henry. *The Works of Henry Clay*, New York: Barnes & Burr, 1863.

Cutler, William G. "Territorial History," *History of the State of Kansas*, Chicago: A. T. Andreas, 1883. www.kan coll.org/books/cutler/terrhist/terrhist-p2.html

Ehrlich, Walter. *They Have No Rights: Dred Scott's Struggle for Freedom*, Westport, CT: Greenwood Press, 1979.

Forbes, Robert Pierce. *The Missouri Compromise and Its Aftermath*, Chapel Hill, NC: University of North Carolina Press, 2007.

Johnson, Charles W. *How Our Laws Are Made*, Washington, D.C.: Governmental Printing Office, 1998.

King, Rufus, and Charles Rufus King. *The Life and Correspondence of Rufus King*, New York: G. P. Putnam's Sons, 1899.

Loeb, Isidor. *Constitutions and Constitutional Conventions in Missouri*, Columbia, Missouri: State Historical Society of Missouri, 1920.

Monroe, James. *The Writings of James Monroe: Including a Collection of His Public and Private Papers and Correspondence Now for the First Time Printed*, New York: G. P. Putnam's Sons, 1902.

Sprague, John Francis. *Journal of Maine History*, vol. 10, 1913. Library of Congress. www.archive.org/stream/spraguesjournalo10spra/spraguesjournalo10spra_djvu.txt

Waugh, John C. *On the Brink of Civil War*, Lanham, MD: Rowman & Littlefield, 2003.

U.S. COURT CASES

McCulloch v. *Maryland*, 17 U.S. 316 (1819).

Winny v. *Whitesides*, 1 Mo. 472(1824). Missouri Supreme Court.

Rachel v. *Walker*, 4 Mo. 350, 354 (1836). Missouri Supreme Court.

Dred Scott, a man of color v. *Irene Emerson*, St. Louis Circuit Court Records, Nov. 1846, case #1.

Harriet Scott, a woman of color v. *Emerson*, St. Louis Circuit Court Records, Nov. 1846, case #2.

Scott v. *Emerson*, 15 Mo. 576, 586 (1852).
Scott v. *Emerson*, 15 Mo. 576, 586 (1852), Justice Hamilton Gamble, *dissenting*.

Scott v. *Sandford*, 60 U.S. 393 (1857).

U.S. Documents

"An Act to Organize the Territories of Nebraska and Kansas." *United States Statutes at Large: Treaties of the United States of America*, v. 10, Boston: Little Brown, 1855, 277. www.vlib.us/amdocs/texts/kanneb.html

Annals of Congress: Debates and Proceedings, 1789–1824. http://memory.loc.gov/ammem/amlaw/lwaclink.html

Appendix to the *Congressional Globe*, 33rd Congress, 1st session, 1850.

Congressional Globe: Debates and Proceedings, 1833–1873. http://memory.loc.gov/ammem/amlaw/lwcglink.html

Jefferson, Thomas. *Papers.* ME 6:388, Papers 12:440. http://etext.virginia.edu/jefferson/texts

University of Nebraska Press/University of Nebraska–Lincoln Libraries–Electronic Text Center (March 2005). *The Journals of the Lewis and Clark Expedition.* http://lewisandclarkjournals.unl.edu/read/?_xmlsrc=1806-09-23.xml&_xslsrc=LCstyles.xsl

Websites

Administrative Office of the U.S. Courts
www.uscourts.gov

American Memory
http://memory.loc.gov/ammem/index.html

Avalon Project at Yale Law School
www.yale.edu/lawweb/avalon/amerdoc/bank-tj.htm

From Revolution to Reconstruction
www.let.rug.nl/usa

The Lincoln-Douglas Debates of 1858
www.nps.gov/liho/historyculture/debates.htm

National Archives
www.archives.gov

Oyez Project: U.S. Supreme Court Multimedia Website
www.oyez.org

U.S. Constitution Online
www.usconstitution.net/consttop_fedr.html

All websites accessible as of October 3, 2009.

Index

Page numbers in **boldface** are illustrations, tables, and charts.

About the Author

SUSAN DUDLEY GOLD has worked as a reporter for a daily newspaper, managing editor of two statewide business magazines, and freelance writer for several regional publications. She has written more than four dozen books for middle-school and high-school students on a variety of topics, including American history, health issues, law, and space.

Gold has won numerous awards for her work, including most recently the selection of Loving *v.* Virginia: *Lifting the Ban Against Interracial Marriage*, part of Marshall Cavendish's Supreme Court Milestones series, as one of the Notable Social Studies Trade Books for Young People in 2009. Two other books in that series were recognized in 2008: United States *v.* Amistad: *Slave Ship Mutiny*, selected as a Carter G. Woodson Honor Book, and Tinker *v.* Des Moines: *Free Speech for Students*, awarded first place in the National Federation of Press Women's communications contest, nonfiction juvenile book category.

Gold has written a number of titles in the Landmark Legislation series for Marshall Cavendish. She is the author of several books on Maine history. She and her husband, John Gold, own and operate a web design and publishing business in Maine. They have one son, Samuel, and one granddaughter, Callie Samantha.